Waking Up to Your Self

A Guide to Living Your Truth

Waking Up to Your Self

A Guide to Living Your Truth

Patrick Marando

BOOKS

Winchester, UK
Washington, USA

First published by O-Books, 2024
O-Books is an imprint of Collective Ink Ltd.,
Unit 11, Shepperton House, 89 Shepperton Road, London, N1 3DF
office@collectiveinkbooks.com
www.collectiveinkbooks.com
www.o-books.com

For distributor details and how to order please visit the 'Ordering' section on our website.

ISBN: 978 1 80341 531 4
978 1 80341 538 3 (ebook)
Library of Congress Control Number: 2023934563

A CIP catalogue record for this book is available from the British Library.

Design: Lapiz Digital Services

UK: Printed and bound by CPI Group (UK) Ltd, Croydon, CR0 4YY
Printed in North America by CPI GPS partners

Contents

Preface

When I was in high school, I decided I wanted to become a psychologist. I was always the person in my class listening to and advising people in need. I seemed to have a logical mind and was apparently good at sharing it, although I was sometimes baffled about why those around me did not seem to see the logical answers I did and were so clouded by their emotions. Maybe it was natural for me to be like this, or perhaps it was how I was raised. So, true to my word I enrolled in a psychology course at university and have been studying and working with the human mind ever since.

Once I began working as a psychologist, I decided it was time to start an exercise program. After speaking to some friends, I began kung fu lessons at a local center. I had been raised Catholic, attended a Catholic school for most of my life, and believed in God, but it was at the martial arts center where I was properly introduced to the idea of chi and life-force energy. This was my first taste of spirituality and I wanted to know more, so I researched everything I could about spirituality, meditation, and mindfulness and combined this acquired knowledge within my own journey of self-awareness. I went on silent meditation retreats and spent hour upon hour in quiet contemplation about myself and life.

It was during this time that a friend introduced me to a spiritual teacher who had studied the practice of Zen and discussed the idea of enlightenment. Although he was in America and I was in Australia, I read his books, listened to his talks online, and even traveled around the world to do meditation retreats with him. By my own private contemplation and realizing his teachings, I woke up to myself—my *true self*, that is. I discovered there was an awareness part of me (and everyone) that is always present, witnessing my body, emotions, and thoughts and possessing an innate wisdom.

While this experience left me forever changed, I was still quite logical and tended toward numbness when it came to emotions. My emotional life consisted of minor happy times and minor sad times, but I mostly abided in the neutral. At first, I thought this was just me; I was wired this way. But after a while, I grew confused and even a bit disillusioned—I had studied psychology, was working as a psychologist, and was practicing the skills I had learned and taught to my clients, yet my emotional state never really shifted.

After a few more years of being in the neutral state, I found a community around me that shared my interests in personal and spiritual growth. Until then I had traveled most of my spiritual journey in relative isolation, and although I learned a lot, I had no one to speak with and personally assist me with any questions I had or problems I faced. It was during one particular conversation with a friend that I had another profound realization: *I was a master at attempting to control my emotions, and this "mastery" prevented me from feeling.* It was a habit begun in childhood and compounded by what I had learned in my studies and job. That is when I began a new phase: having an emotional life and developing my awareness and knowledge of how I was skilled at attempting to control my emotions and only acting out of supposed logic. I understood logic had a part to play as a useful tool in my life, yet it was also limiting when it disconnected me from my true self.

The second phase of my journey led to many emotionally painful but also pleasurable experiences. I searched deeper within and really got to know myself. I traveled to places like Uluru, the Daintree Rainforest, Zen temples in Japan, the Netherlands, Bali, and rural Mongolia. I met spiritual teachers in many disciplines, all in the name of understanding my true self and how it functioned within/as me.

It was during this time that I started a side job as a spiritual teacher. People had begun seeking me out to ask spiritual questions—not just psychological ones—because they wanted to find themselves and *their* unique path. It was through a combination of learning and teaching (both psychology and spirituality) that I ultimately developed a clearer picture of my true self and how it was guiding me to live. *I had finally woken up to myself.* Until then, my logical mind had governed my journey, but now I was able to understand my emotions and respect how they motivated me toward my deepest satisfaction and connection with my truest desires—the desires of my true self.

This is not a religious book, but it is based upon spirituality, which I understand as the nature of reality itself. While I continue to learn and connect to my true self on deeper levels, it is from my discoveries as a truth seeker, spiritual teacher, and psychologist that I wrote this step-by-step guide to being human. I hope this book will guide you as you discover your true self, learn how to utilize your emotions and mind for your greatest benefit, and wake up to that self.

Patrick

Acknowledgements

My deepest gratitude and appreciation to my family. You have taught me so much about emotions and my inner truth—more than you could possibly ever realize. Your loving foundation over the years has made this book possible.

To my dear friend Pam, I cannot thank you enough. I couldn't have written this book without your support and guiding wisdom. You truly are a gift to me and to the world.

To those who offered me advice in the writing process, thank you very much for your time and efforts.

To Adyashanti, you have been a guide from afar. Your words and teachings have helped lead me to my inner truth.

To my editor, Alice Peck. Your gift for words and guidance through uncharted waters has helped me immensely.

Finally, to my many guides, teachers, and students along my path. Thank you, thank you, thank you. No one person held the key to bringing me the wisdom of this book, but with each of you I was given great direction, vast compassion, and an ability to look within with clearer insight.

Introduction

Welcome to you! Yes, you, the true "you" beneath your conditioned mind and full identification with your body. It is for this "you" that I wrote this book—a book about remembering who you really are, a book about living from your true self, about remembering how to love yourself and live freely.

This is a book about understanding how the mind develops, works, and does not always align with your true self. It is a book about learning how to understand your beliefs and utilize your mind to help (instead of limit) you. It is about getting to know your emotions, understanding why you have each one of them, and seeing how they can enhance your life when aligned with your true self. It is a book about recognizing conditioned thoughts and the behaviors you have learned in a (sometimes misguided) attempt to help you feel better or safer. It is a book about having awareness of these attempts and deciding to use our minds in a way that allows us to live a better, freer life.

Most of all, it is a book about growing your light so that you embrace life as your true self, fully awaken to who you are, and live from this state—not a debilitating one that causes suffering, but a state of wellbeing, peace, and fulfillment.

SECTION 1

What Is the True Self?

Chapter One

Introduction to the True Self

Do you know who you really are?

No, not your name, but who you are underneath that name, underneath your beliefs about yourself? Who you are in the space between your thoughts. Your internal being that is independent of culture, gender, sexual orientation, or appearance. Your core self underlying your temperament and personality who is witness to all the roles you play. The part that endures throughout your entire life no matter how your physical self changes. The *you* who knows your deepest wants and desires and exactly how to reach them or allow them to emerge. *Who are you?*

When I was about 20 years old, I definitely did not know who I really was, although I was beginning to become aware of how I behaved differently in different settings. In general, with my family I was quite easygoing and well behaved, with my friends I swung from outgoing and silly to serious, and with new people I was extremely polite and on the reserved side. Being aware of these differences led to me ask, "Who am I really? What is my true personality?" I wracked my brain so often and for so long to find this answer, but couldn't. I kept discovering that my behavior was dynamic and the personality traits I displayed in any given situation changed. Unbeknown to me, at the time, was that my personality encompassed all those qualities. Not only that, a part of me was aware of my personality and behaviors as they were occurring and aware of every single change in me that had ever occurred in my life. *The real me.*

Chances are, like the 20-year-old me, you do not know the "you" I am talking about either, at least not very well. I'm talking about the real you, your true self.

The thing is, it is not that you do not know this you. What is more accurate is that you have forgotten this part of you existed and most likely have forgotten how to listen to or identify with it. This may be because you have been unwittingly deceived by your parents, caregivers, and members of society who taught you in the same way they were taught. Not out of malice, but rather ignorance. They did not know any better and only taught you about who they thought you to be.

The deception starts at birth. As humans we are born as our true self within a body. But this does not include a belief that our body is our "self." We are born as pure awareness within a body, and we are taught from the beginning to identify with it as our self. I call these taught beliefs the "egoic conditioned self." The egoic conditioned self consists of the learned beliefs that we are our body, our emotional states, and our mind. This egoic conditioned self begins when we are given a name and repeatedly called that name throughout the life of our body. We identify with the name as ourselves. But what we are naming as "self" is an illusion. No static state of self exists. We are taught by those around us to believe our body is our "self," even though our body is constantly changing and remains in constant flux throughout our lives.

The next thing we are often taught is to believe that our emotional states are the same as our "self." "I *am* angry" or "I *am* sad." We lose the awareness that they are experiences being noticed within our field of awareness which come and go, despite our true self remaining constant. Subsequently we identify with our mind and its beliefs *as* ourselves. We may say, *I am a good person...* or *I am a bad person... I am a Christian...* or *I am a Buddhist... I am a funny person... I am a perfectionist...*

I am a worrier... These belief patterns cannot be who we really are; they are labels of the mind that come and go while our awareness remains.

While this static state of self does not exist, identifying as our self through our body, emotions, or our mind is not all bad. This identification can assist us with functioning. If we never identified with these points within awareness, then we would never care for our physical bodies. We would ignore experiences of pain or ease and never listen to and utilize our feelings for making our life better or keeping us safe. We would also never utilize our minds to make our life easier through the wonderful knowledge and information stored in it.

Problematically, identifying with only our bodies, mind, and emotions will lead to suffering and a robotic life-experience. We will be victims or slaves to whatever is happening to our bodies or emotions or whatever our mind happens to be reacting to in the moment.

But what about our spirit—our true self? Did we ever learn to identify with that part? While many of us also have some concept of the spirit within, it is seldom taught, at least not accurately. Hence, our understanding is poor and it remains a mysterious component of us. It is the spirit part that I call the "true self," which, if we know how to live from it, can free us from our identification with pain and suffering, allowing us to live a happy, content, peaceful and harmonious existence. It is the part of us that can help us to transcend our conditioned egoic mind and enter into the peace and bliss of a deep true-self connection.

This may sound promising, or perhaps too good to be true, considering the pain and unhappiness we experience and see in the world. But rest assured, while you may not yet know it or may sense it only as a subtle internal presence, your true self exists as the deepest part of you, gently urging you to connect to who you really are, leading you to a state of deep peace that is unshakable even when life seems difficult.

Many have written and spoken about the true self and most of us have heard at least one version or label. Some people call it spirit, some call it soul, yet it may go by many other names such as the higher self, inner being, super-conscious, wise mind, authentic self, Buddha nature, Christ consciousness, inner awareness, inner essence, consciousness. The true self is a key principle in most religions, but it is not limited to religion. It is connected to spirituality, yet even then it is not limited to spiritual people. The true self is the energetic essence that connects everyone from sinners to saints, from all sexes and genders, from newborns to the elderly, from devout believers to atheists, and is shared by all races and nationalities of people. It is the nature of reality itself, the reality flowing through us all.

The true self is an energetic essence, which like a river with many currents, gently guides us toward the path of smoothest flow. Of course all of our paths are not the same. We each have our own river and currents to follow, but we have the choice at any given moment to connect to the current we specifically align with and float with or fight against that current.

Discovering Your True Self

In actuality our true self has never gone anywhere. It is our purpose as human beings to live from this state of self, to live in the flow of our truth. For some of us this happens instinctively, for others instantaneously upon realization, and for others still, it emerges gradually and develops over time. Our true self, though, has always been and will forever be with us and part of us. It is the center of our being, the very core of our existence. Perhaps you recall having a surreal out-of-body experience where you were acutely aware of everything going on within and around you? This is a time when you were in the state of awareness of the true self and witness to your body, mind, and emotions.

When we were born, we were born as the pure awareness (our true self) within our bodies and our raw self (our instincts, innate personality, temperament, and reactions to life situations) built into our bodies. We were not born with thought patterns or beliefs or any identification with our body as being us. While we had awareness of physical sensations and responded to them, we did not identify with them.

The identification comes as we grow. Someone, most likely a parent, gives us a name. We learn to identify with the named body we are in and treat it as who we are. Our body, while constantly changing, is called the same name repeatedly, so our identification with our name as "me" is reinforced. The problem here is that although we do indeed have a body, our spirit is the center of our being. Our body is not who we are. Our body is a constantly changing organism in perpetual flux. It morphs and shifts around our spirit throughout our lives. Our body replaces every cell every seven years, yet our inner awareness remains the same. It is the silent watcher beneath the surface of our body, noticing not only the changes in our body but also the changes in the world and environment. So, my body was named Patrick when I was born and here I am now as an adult still named Patrick even though I have a completely different body from the one I was born with, a body that remains in a state of change.

Not only do we learn to identify with our body, but we soon learn to identify with our conditioned egoic minds (emotional states and thoughts) as us. We learn we are what we are thinking or feeling, when in essence the thinking and feeling is happening within our state of awareness. Our true self is aware of the perceptions and emotions coming and going. In fact, our emotions (like the cells in our bodies) are forever changing and our beliefs have the potential to change as well if we want to change them or if life shows us another way.

In other words, we exist with a mind and body, which our true self forever witnesses. The true self underlies every feeling and belief we have ever had; it exists even when our mind is empty of thought and we are not experiencing any particular emotions. To return to the example of my 20-year-old self, I was identifying as my personality, but as it was different in different situations this identification led to my confusion about who I was, because there was always a part of me present no matter which aspect of my personality arose. And even identifying as being confused (an emotion) was not accurate because that part of me remained when clarity replaced confusion.

If you are aware enough, and sit within yourself long enough, you may intuitively rediscover the part of you that has not changed throughout your life, the part of you that has been silently watching, silently aware of everything you have experienced, from bodily changes, to the five senses—sights, sounds, smells, tastes, touch—to situations, to thoughts, emotions and actions. The true self has noticed these things arise, was there during them, and remains when they have disappeared or changed. It is the part of us that continues to exist when our body dies, our eternal essence.

Our true self silently observes, but that is not the only thing it does. The true self gently motivates us to live from its perspective, one of peace and love. It softly urges us to wake up to it and act from that part of ourselves, to change how we perceive things, and to bring our view of the world more clearly in alignment with it. It summons us to live from it and not solely from the conditioned egoic mind. This inner essence runs through each of us in the same way, although the motivating behavior is unique to each individual. It is trying to get us to transcend our conditioned mind so we can live in the joy and harmony of the true self. While we may still feel pleasant or unpleasant emotions, living as our true selves means we do not believe things that do not align with it, and we no longer *identify* those emotions or beliefs as who we are. We allow them all to exist and decide if they serve us as points on an internal compass directing us toward or away from the things we truly want or do not want.

Some people will wake up to their true self instantaneously without any effort, but for most of us it will require some conscious effort. While we cannot force the realization, we can grow our awareness of it and our reconnection to it. We can learn how it communicates and motivates us into action. It communicates with us through our emotions, intuitive thoughts, and overall intuition.

We can gain deeper connection to our true self by growing our awareness of our raw self and our conditioned egoic mind. This means understanding our innate responses and also our beliefs and emotional responses, as well as understanding the behavioral habits we have developed and the motivations for using them. The more we do this, the more we will be able to differentiate our true self from our raw and conditioned self and thus be able to connect to the true part of ourselves at any given moment, despite whatever may be going on internally with our mind or body or externally with situations we face.

Our emotions are our entry points to our belief systems and at any given moment they can reflect the depth of our connection to our true self. The better we feel, the more likely it is that we are in alignment with our true self; the worse we feel, the less likely we are in alignment. So, when I am feeling peace or at ease, it is more likely that I am living aligned with my true self than when I am feeling anxious or stressed—although in saying this, our true self is at peace even when we may be experiencing unpleasant emotions.

The urges of the true self do not always follow the logic or reason of the conditioned mind. Instead, this is a dynamic essence shifting or changing the urges and impulses within us at any given moment to best suit the situation at hand and the overall flow of life. It does so with the intention of motivating us to live the life we truly want.

Before we can understand how the true self communicates to us, it is important to better understand what constitutes the true self. The true self is pure awareness or energy combined with wisdom. The energy is part of and connected to all that is in the entirety of existence. It is composed of pure love, not the romantic type, but rather a deep inner state of connection and oneness with all that is. This means the true self abides beyond the world of opposites. It is always in a state of loving everything and everyone as if they were an extension of us (because they are). The true self always exists in this moment. It is not present in the past or future, but in the eternal now which is the very moment in time we are engaged with. It is continuously allowing and accepting of everything. It does not need anything to be changed, improved, or bettered to be content or at peace. It is also self-loving, self-compassionate, and self-accepting and extends these sentiments to all others.

Our true self is wise beyond belief. It knows us better than our mind knows us. It is aware of the true nature of reality. It is also aware of our deepest wants and desires and knows everything needed to make them happen. Its perspective on life or situations is often different from the perspective of our conditioned mind. Its perspective will often make us experience a sense of peace or acceptance about what is occurring and it could even motivate us to take inspired aligned action to change what is occurring. It has a unique balance of knowing when inaction or action is required for the most desired outcomes. It approaches situations through love (whether of self or others).

It also communicates in an encouraging way and knows that everything is a constantly evolving process; nothing is ever stuck or stagnant. It is willing to experience any emotional discomforts so that they do not get in the way of it expressing its gentle pull toward our truest wants. Our true self knows the answers to our questions and can provide them when they are most apt and useful for us. It communicates this information through emotions, thoughts, intuition, urges, bodily sensations, and gut feelings. While listening to the true self is normal for children, many (maybe even most) of us have long forgotten how to do this, and so we need to remember or relearn how to communicate with the true self.

To do so we must first realize how our true self functions and communicates with us, what our beliefs are, and our emotional states and their causes. Our true self can communicate through our intuitive thoughts and emotional states, motivating us to either change our belief patterns to realign with it or act upon them to create the life we truly want. The only issue is our raw and conditioned egoic self will also communicate through our thoughts and emotions and may not be giving us the best advice for a particular situation.

Our job is to learn how to differentiate between true-self thoughts and emotions and the raw and conditioned egoic thoughts and emotions. To do so we must first understand what causes emotions and how beliefs that differ from or conflict with our true self are created in our minds.

Chapter Two

Genesis of Emotions

As a child I remember being very sensitive emotionally to what was going on around me. If someone shouted at me, I would cringe in hurt or disapproval. I felt very sad at seeing people in pain. I didn't know it at the time, but it was my inborn sensitivity that led me to develop a strategy of shutting down my emotions. Making a choice to become numb meant self-preservation and minimizing my overall pain. This numbness protected me, but it also resulted in me becoming a more emotionally diminished adult after the strategy no longer served me.

Emotions are the cornerstones of our lives as human beings. They function as internal compasses, often guiding and motivating us to behave in ways most aligned with our true self. They offer us a point of relativity, calling us back to who we truly are when we disconnect from our true state of peace or contentment. Without them, our lives would be bland, boring, and hollow. We would feel no connection with others and be unable to relate to anyone. We would have no impetus to do anything. We would not even know what we liked or disliked. We would have no ability to function in our day-to-day lives without them and would even likely be dead without some. Whether we like it or not, we cannot live a fulfilling life without the entire spectrum of emotions we feel. They add flavor to our lives, they trigger us to remember who we truly are, and assist us by creating a sense of direction toward the wants of the true self.

We are born with our emotions intact, and as we grow, our emotions will not allow us to sit idly as our life passes by. They are there to guide us and motivate us either toward what we want or like, or away from what we do not want or dislike. They are there to help us find connection and purpose, to remind us how far or close we are to our true self at any given moment. And when used and utilized with such simplicity they have the ability to keep us on a path of peace, contentment, and joy—helping us find ourselves and create our life to be exactly how we truly desire it to be.

This view of emotions may seem idealistic, because so many people struggle with their feelings. We live in a world where stress, depression, and anxiety are more common than ever before. People are stuck in vicious loops of suffering and enduring the pain of their feelings with no reprieve. Or maybe they are so avoidant of certain feelings, they withdraw from living a rich full life of the true self in favor of a restricted life of minimized emotional pain and pleasure, leading to feelings of discontent.

Naturally, everyone wants to be content. None of us want to feel the pain that comes with life. Our conditioned egoic mind wants us to feel either pleasure or a sense of security. The true self is not solely concerned by this; it knows which emotions are and are not required in every situation. It also knows a life of only pleasure is not a realistic approach and would not benefit us if we were to live without emotional pain and only unchallenged security. It wants us to use our emotions to serve us and remind us of who we really are. Hence it communicates through emotions (pleasant or unpleasant) which motivate us to act in the most aligned way possible at any given time. However, our egoic conditioned mind does this as well—it can also trigger emotions to motivate us toward or away from actions that best serve it.

I divide emotions into two categories: shadow and light. The *shadow* emotions are the unpleasant ones, the ones we try our best to control and have as seldom as possible. The *light* emotions are those we like, the ones that feel pleasant and which we try to have as much as possible. Just as shadow requires light to exist, emotional pleasure is only possible with the relative point of emotional pain.

Without the emotional pain which comes with life, without our shadow emotions, we would not be able to find or appreciate the emotional pleasure—light emotions—which can be a large part of our lives. It can be our shadow that motivates us to move toward the light emotions of our true self. For example, we would not feel happiness without the relative point of feeling sad. We must have the contrasting emotion if we are to know the existence or intensity of its opposite emotion. Plus, it is the sadness that can motivate and assist us to do the things to bring about the opposing emotion of happiness. Our job is to learn how to listen to our emotions so we can understand them while also listening to the wisdom of our true self. To do so, we must first understand what emotions are and what each one is attempting to communicate.

What Are Emotions?

In short, emotions are energetic impulses within us that manifest as feelings or physical sensations in our bodies. As humans we have given these physical sensations labels such as fear, sadness, loneliness, or anger. We get these names from those around us. When we are children, our emotional reactions to situations are a result of our temperament, genetics, or biological makeup. This is our raw self, the innate part of us having inborn emotional reactions. Then (if we are lucky) our parents or caregivers give us a name for the emotion. While a name may be helpful in identifying emotions, the name is *not* the emotion itself. Thus, we grow up with an idea of the name of an emotion, rather than what it physiologically represents in our bodies.

It is in the labeling process where debates occur as to how many emotions we have as humans and which one a person may be feeling. Emotions are subjective and only the person feeling them can truly know what they are experiencing within their body, whether they have a name/label for it or not. In this book, though, I will label, categorize, and offer my understanding of the most commonly experienced emotions.

Before I go there, though, it is important to understand what causes emotions, that is, what creates the physiological changes in our bodies. Beyond the urges of our true self triggering them, there are two primary causes for emotions. The first is our innate biology and genetic makeup, which constitutes our raw self. The second is the beliefs or perceptions we hold within our conditioned egoic mind, our conditioned egoic self. These two causes tend to bounce off each other and compound any emotions we are feeling. Our job is to learn when they serve to help us hear the calling of the true self and when they do not.

Chapter Three

Causes of Emotions

I have spoken to many people who feel sad because they are not in a relationship. Sometimes it is an innate cause of sadness and other times it is an egoic cause. As far as evolution goes, having this innate sadness can help motivate us to build or grow connections to others so that we can form a relationship to evolutionarily increase our chance of survival and having offspring. While we may experience the innate form of sadness about a lack of relationship, there are also many people who feel sad because of what they have learned to believe. They may feel sad because they have learned they are not good enough if they are single, they have failed if they do not get married, or perhaps they believe that a relationship is not possible for them. This type of sadness arises from the things we have been taught that become conditioned in our egoic mind. Often, our innate emotions will then interact with our conditioned ones and create more suffering.

Innate Causes of Emotions: The Raw Self

While our belief systems trigger many of our emotions, we are all born as a raw self, with innate emotional responses within our bodies. While they may not all be readily available to us as babies, they are programmed within our genetic imprint to come out as we grow. The reason being that they are designed to help us function and motivate us to survive but also to help us move our life in a better direction.

The main areas of our brain responsible for our emotions are the limbic and the autonomic nervous systems. We inherit the genes that make up these systems from our parents. As well as these systems, we can inherit the emotional sensitivities that come with this genetic and biological makeup. Because every person has a unique set of genetics, our brains will respond differently to one another within situations, thus will not always trigger the same emotional reactions or intensity within us all. Many babies and children (just like adults) experiencing the same situations will respond with different emotions or intensities of emotion. For example, one child might be terrified by a noise while another might not react or will react only mildly. Or perhaps a child might feel shy and anxious with new people where another is confident and calm. The reason for these initial reactions is our genetic or innate temperamental disposition and our personal biology. Because as young children we have not yet learned to perceive the world, we are responding to it as our raw self, from our inbuilt emotional sensitivities which differ between us. Hence, we all come into the world at differing emotional levels and not as a blank slate.

We also need our emotions for our survival and to help direct our behavior and lives. Our instinctual internally programmed "fight, flight, or freeze" response protects us from danger. When faced with a possible threat, our body goes through certain changes to either fight or flee from the threat, or freeze in response to the threat. Another example of innate emotions is when we lose something important or meaningful; it is natural to experience sadness or grief. Or when we are shouted at by a parent, we feel disapproved of.

While many emotions are instinctual and innate responses within us occurring from our raw self, we also have emotions that are triggered due to the beliefs we have learned within the conditioned egoic mind.

Emotions Caused by Beliefs and Thinking Patterns: The Conditioned Egoic Self

While we have raw-self emotions, many of our emotional responses are the result of how we see the world, of what we believe or perceive about the world and ourselves. These feelings are created by the conceived notions we have developed through experiences and lessons learned in our lives—in other words through nurture.

If we were to look at ourselves or the world without thought or belief, we would all see the same things. We would appear exactly as we are; the world would appear exactly as it is. Not good or bad, not right or wrong. Think of a newborn baby without any preconceived concept of what we or the world should or should not be. This is how we all were—innocent of ourselves or the world, and free of judgment about the supposed rights and wrongs of ourselves or the world. As children we experienced the innate emotions, the ones not attached to belief patterns. They were natural and in sync with our biological and genetic structure. They derived from our physiological brain structure, temperament, and personality. That is, until we started to learn...

Beliefs or perceptions are repeated thought-patterns in our conditioned egoic mind which we hold as a true representation of ourselves, others, or the world we live in. We then use these beliefs as our filter for how we interpret the world. They are like a lens through which we see the world, rather than seeing the world unfiltered. The lens we have learned to look through determines how we feel about ourselves or a situation. But how did these lenses develop?

I have already discussed origins of the beliefs about our "self," so I am going to focus on beliefs about the world. At first, we learned by the way we felt. If a situation triggered an emotion within us, we soon learned to believe it was either a good or bad situation depending on which one got triggered. We then learned a strategy to cope with the emotion and situation. This is the origin of beliefs and perceptions. We learned what to believe from observing the environment around us. We learned what was true or false, what was right and what was wrong, what was good and what was bad, what was desirable and what was undesirable.

Initially we learned from our experiences. If we were hungry, we cried. If our needs were met, we may have learned that we are important, and that crying was a tool for getting those needs met. While the lesson may not occur on the first occasion, after numerous repeated events a belief or perception will develop. And on it goes: we may cry for attention, and if it is continually given, we develop ideas of entitlement to attention and our self-importance as a being. However, if not given enough attention we may develop beliefs of not being worthy. Beliefs develop within us as we decipher and make sense of our world in order to navigate through it in a way that minimizes our emotional pain.

When babies are born they have no concept of right or wrong, good or bad, true or false. They learn these things from the people around them, their parents, siblings, teachers, family, media, society, religion, and culture. We normally either take on board the beliefs of those around us or reject the beliefs of those around us (we choose the opposite belief) as to whether those beliefs are true or false. Beliefs can often be false. They are inherited—person to person, generation to generation, and society to society despite the absence of criteria to support their truth. If we learn something is good, and we do it or have it, then we experience a pleasant emotion. If we learn something is bad, and we do it or have it, we feel one of the shadow emotions. Because we are children and have no concept of good or bad until we are taught, we believe what we learn, we take it as fact. Those teaching us learned their beliefs in exactly the same way—from their parents or caregivers, who were taught by their parents and caregivers, and so on, as beliefs got passed down and shared.

As children, when we believe something, it feels like a reality, and our emotional response develops from that "reality." If a belief is deemed true, the emotion will follow the belief. If a child is taught their behavior is unacceptable, then they will believe it is bad and they are not good enough, and thus feel unworthy about having that specific behavior, whether there is any truth to it or not. This could then lead to behaviors of rejecting or hating themselves for engaging in that behavior. Although our beliefs continue to grow and evolve over time, as adults we are mostly acting out the beliefs we learned as children and continue to have the emotional responses associated with those beliefs.

Because we have believed them for so long, those emotions feel so real that we feel justified in feeling that way and we remain attached to those habitual belief-patterns. Even if we see the belief as false, simply changing the belief will not change the emotional response attached to it. Our body will instead react emotionally to the old belief. For example, if I am repeatedly taught that I am bad if I am overweight, even though as an adult I know this isn't logical, if I am overweight now I continue to feel not-good-enough because of the lessons I have learned earlier in my life.

In reality there is no such thing as a true belief. Beliefs are thoughts we utilize to describe "reality." Reality exists whether we think about it or not. And yet, some beliefs are more aligned with reality than others, in that they more accurately describe reality, even though they are not the reality itself. You may find this hard to understand. The reason is, we have learned to believe our thoughts as if they were truth, and as a result we have learned to emotionally feel them to be true. This is why we continue to reinforce beliefs whether they serve us or not.

As we grow and have these emotions, we also learn patterns of behavior which attempt to assist us in controlling or avoiding these shadow emotions and attaining the light emotions. These behaviors tend to revolve around the "fight, flight, or freeze" responses and may be either internal, thinking behaviors or external action-based behaviors. The fight, flight or freeze response is an innate emotional pattern that protected us from danger as we evolved as humans, yet it also serves to protect us from feeling certain "threatening" emotions. Because of this we have developed skills to either "fight" against an emotion, "flee" from an emotion, or "freeze up" about an emotion. While many of these resistance, avoidance, or control behaviors are useful in helping us feel better in the short term and develop strategies and tools that can be of assistance to our lives in the long term, overusing these shadow strategies can lead to suffering and a disconnection from our true selves. To avoid emotional pain or enhance emotional pleasure we may end up being what others want us to be and not who we truly are. In a sense, we create our suffering as a reaction to our emotional pain.

As we grow older, we begin to identify with our emotional states. That is, we create our sense of self from the way we feel, such as "I am a happy person" or "I am a depressed person." These beliefs about our self when connected to our emotional states can also lead to much suffering because we will need to exert a level of resistance to release them as we've been conditioned to believe they are who we are.

Another thing we do with our beliefs is reinforce our emotional states. Our beliefs are formed by experiences and the emotions they create. These become the foundation of our expected experiences and provide a sense of security in the familiar emotional state they create. This in turn leads us to subconsciously seek out and create familiar emotional states (be they pleasant or unpleasant) as a means of feeling secure in the world. This can often result in seeking out or subconsciously creating the emotions we want least, because of the familiarity and security they supposedly represent.

Many of us are unaware of our emotions or that we may be trying to control them, let alone that we are causing our own suffering. We have been attempting to control emotions or identifying with them for so long that those habits are ingrained in us, and we feel they are who we are. This could not be further from the truth. The ingrained version of you is conditioned egoic self—the version of you that thinks and behaves in certain ways to chase, avoid, get rid of, or identify with certain emotional responses. The part of you that lives via your programming whether it serves you or not. The part that learned to survive with the least amount of shadow pain possible. The part of you disconnected from the real you, your true self.

In a sense we develop a personality that is not our true personality; we develop a conditioned personality out of a desire to not have or cope with the shadow emotions at all costs, or to identify with those emotions as ourselves no matter the cost. We develop a robotic type of personality which does not allow us free choice to think, act, or behave in a dynamic way that is the way to the true self. Instead, it causes us to continue to habitually re-enact belief and behavior patterns we learned as children, despite different circumstances always occurring.

Why do we do this? Why do we continue to act the same way?

The primary reason is we have forgotten who we really are. We have forgotten about our true self and how it speaks to us. We have disconnected from our abilities to listen to its advice and behave accordingly. Instead, we have focused on our conditioned egoic self, whose primary drive is to keep itself relevant by motivating us to only have the pleasant (light) emotions, and to avoid feeling the unpleasant (shadow) ones. It wants us to feel good at all costs. Thus, we will behave in ways that give us the short-term hit of feeling better, despite the longer-term outcome of making us feel worse. Despite how often we may have used those control or resistance strategies because they worked or were useful in the past and sometimes work now, we continue to use them in an attempt to attain the light and keep the conditioned egoic mind from the metaphorical death it fears. Overusing these behavior patterns in turn disconnects us from our true self—our inner wisdom and decisions about how to deal with emotions and situations in our lives. This leads to further suffering.

Emotions Caused by the True Self

Our true self will also cause emotions to trigger within us. The current of our specific river will gently pull us toward it, and the true self will utilize our feelings to motivate us toward action that truly aligns with its flow. Whether it be to chase something, avoid something, or even to trigger an emotion to purge ourselves of whatever emotional baggage we are carrying. Our true self knows our desires and it knows the exact emotional trigger to assist us in creating action it is aligned with. The true self also has the wisdom, though, to not follow emotional actions that are based solely on the raw self or the conditioned egoic mind.

Our overall goal is to rebuild our connection to our true self and, by doing so, escape the robotic suffering nature of the conditioned egoic self and our raw self. When we do, we free ourselves from the loop of conditioned beliefs, emotional reactions, and behaviors, and find our deepest and most true desires in every situation. This connection allows us to live and rest in our natural state of wellbeing, peace, and contentment that is our true self.

However, to hear our true self we must first learn to recognize the times we hold a belief pattern that differs from the one held by the true self. Our emotional states are great guides of when this occurs. If we feel a shadow emotion, it may be an indicator that our belief patterns are unaligned with those of our true nature. This can motivate us to change our belief patterns to realign with that deepest part of us. When we have aligned our beliefs we'll feel lighter and more peaceful about a situation.

SECTION 2

Aligning with the True Self

Chapter Four

Lighter Perceptions and Beliefs

Our perceptions and beliefs color the way we see ourselves and the world. They are the lens through which we interpret every experience. Whatever we believe about ourselves or within any situation is going to become the reality of that situation and thus lead us to feel the belief as true. Often, though, the perceptions or beliefs of the conditioned egoic mind do not match up with the beliefs of the true self. When this is the case, we are often lost in an illusion or one-sided view of reality—often the types of perception which cause us to suffer. As mentioned, there is no such thing as a true belief, though some thoughts point to a closer truth than others. Being aware of this is the first step toward changing how we see ourselves and the world and aligning our belief systems with our true self.

The best way to know we are having heavy, less aligned perceptions is to pay attention to the shadow emotions. Often the beliefs we have within a situation will be the triggers of our emotional responses. Mostly when we are having unhelpful, darker, or heavy thoughts we will feel unpleasant and more of the shadow emotions. On the flipside, when we feel the light ones, there is a high chance our beliefs are aligned, brighter, or more helpful for us. Sometimes, even if we are not having any perception within a situation, we will have emotions. When we experience these types of shadow emotion, we are likely going to get shadowy heavier, less aligned thoughts that accompany it. This leads to more of the same emotion, if not layers of other unpleasant emotions. Just like when we are feeling lighter emotions, we tend to have lighter perceptions. Hence beliefs can trigger emotions, which can then trigger perceptions and beliefs.

This may cause an upward spiral of feeling lighter and lighter and a deeper connection to our true self, or a downward spiral of feeling heavier and heavier and a pinched-off connection to our true self.

An example of a downward spiral for me was when I felt disappointed about quitting kung fu before reaching the highest level. I believed I should have done better, then started asking myself: *Why didn't I do better? I should have completed all the levels. What's wrong with me? I'm terrible at this.* When I did this, not only did I feel disappointed, but the thoughts and perceptions of my egoic mind spiraled me down into anger, frustration, and self-hate. An upward spiral might have been more along the lines of having perceptions such as: *Yes, I feel disappointed, but I tried my best. I have done a good job to do it for this long. I have learned a lot and it has added much value to my life. My body is asking me to stop; it's okay to listen to it.* Thinking this way might not eliminate my disappointment but it would mean I would not feel worse and could be more at peace with the situation. Our overall goal is to create an upward spiral of beliefs to bridge toward those of the true self.

Many of us know this. If I believe my glass is half full I'm likely to feel better about my situation than if I perceive the glass as half empty. A lot of people in our lives have told us to think positively and we will feel better. Feeling better or being at ease are two indicators of connection with our true self. All we have to do is choose beliefs that make us feel better.

This is often more easily said than done. You may have tried to change your perceptions in the past, yet no matter what you did, you could not quite believe what you were saying to yourself and they would not stick. It was as if logically you knew the new belief to be true, but emotionally it felt like a lie. It is at this point where we usually hit a snag and give up changing our beliefs, and then keep reinforcing the original beliefs we had.

The reason being that our conditioned beliefs are too far away from the perceptions of the true self. That is, what we *learned* to be true and have consequently reinforced in our lives feels truer than a perception we have only started to connect or reconnect with.

If we cannot believe the thought, we will stop thinking it. Compare this to having spent your whole life in dark or dim light; even though brighter lighting might offer you more experiences, every time someone turns the light on it hurts your eyes, so you turn it off again. We choose to stay in the dark because the contrast with the light is too stark. Instead of turning the light to its brightest setting, our goal is to gradually increase the brightness. The same applies to our heavy beliefs—gradually increase the brightness so that you can bear their weight without the need to reject them. Thus, we gradually bridge our old perceptions toward those of the true self, so at any given moment we are able to look at any situation in a lighter way which makes us feel more at ease, peaceful, accepting or even content about a situation.

To do so often takes practice. It can be difficult to change a belief to its opposite, so gradual credible perceptions are the best way to go. Our goal is to find the lightest, most believable perceptions we can in any situation we find ourselves feeling bad in. Often the worse we feel, the more it would serve us to choose general and less light thoughts; but the better we feel, the easier it will be to choose specific and very light thoughts. If you sense any tension or resistance to any perception you choose, you have probably chosen one which is too far from your conditioned egoic mind, and you may have to change some words to help make it more believable to you. If the perception makes you feel worse, then you have probably chosen one that is too heavy and reinforcing your emotional pain.

Perceptions and beliefs can be difficult to discover. They are stealthy and we are often unaware we are having a perception in any given moment. It is like wearing glasses and forgetting we are looking through a lens. So, instead of looking out for perceptions, our goal is to look out for emotions first, then look to see what our perceptions may be in connection with them. Once you are aware of your heavy perceptions you can make a conscious choice to change them to align more closely with your true self's perception. The more you do this, the lighter they will grow over time.

During the time when I started to choose lighter thoughts I was driving in pouring rain. There were no cars on the road, and I felt free to drive home without any hindrance. That's when a beginning driver pulled in front of me at a roundabout and started driving slowly. As you can imagine, I felt stuck, restricted, and frustrated about the situation. My mind started saying things like: *What is this guy on the road for? He should get off the road. It's too dangerous for a beginner to be driving in this weather.* My true self knew it was okay for a learner driver to be on the road, and it also knew it was fine for me to be behind this learner. I listened to my true self, but this triggered a lot of resistance. My true self was saying something entirely different from what my conditioned self was saying. Because what my conditioned self was saying was causing me to suffer unnecessarily, I decided to choose thoughts that started to bridge the gap between my conditioned egoic mind and my true self. I chose beliefs I could believe, like:

I like the idea of getting home safe—I like being a safe driver.
I enjoy seeing people learn and achieve their goals.
Everyone has to start somewhere.
I like it when people give me space to learn and grow.

When I started thinking this way, I felt better about being behind the beginning driver, even though some frustration still remained. I bridged the gap a little between my conditioned self and my true self.

I was not concerned whether my original beliefs were true or not; I was more concerned with how they made me feel. While it is normal for me to have the conditioned response in the situation, I chose to think lighter and connect deeper to my true self and not perpetuate unhelpful heavy perceptions. When we do this, not only do we tend to feel lighter, but when it comes to a course of action (if one is required) we have greater ability to choose it from the state of our true self. Shifting to a lighter perception not only offers us some relief but also is a key to entering into the wisdom of the true self and choosing the course of action that it is suggesting for us in any given moment.

When you are in a situation where you notice unpleasant feelings, it is useful to try to discover what beliefs or perceptions you habitually hold within a situation. Maybe even write down how you would describe that situation to another person. This will highlight your beliefs. Once you discover them, you can decide to then change those perceptions to make them lighter. Some examples of lighter thoughts are below. They start from somewhat light and general to very light and specific. See if you can notice your beliefs or perceptions when you have shadow emotions, and then see how you go using these thoughts to lighten how you feel (or at least not make it heavier). Try to find at least eight lighter perceptions about the situation so as not to get stuck in your emotional states and create a deeper connection to your true self.

I like the idea of...
It would/could be nice if...
The thought of...feels good to me.

It is possible that...
It could be an opportunity for me to grow...
It might be useful if...
It could benefit me to...
I am looking forward to when...
It is normal for...
It would be useful to...
It would benefit me to...
I am hopeful that...
I like it when...
It helps me when...
I'm in the process of...
I am confident that...
I like feeling...
It will definitely happen...
I love it when...
I am...
I appreciate that...
It's exciting to think...
I can trust that...
I love that...

The more we practice these types of perceptions, the easier it is for us to connect and live from the point of view of our true self and thus be more content and peaceful despite what is going on in the world around us. To listen to what the true self is saying, though, it is important to know how to connect to it.

Chapter Five

Consciously Connecting to Your True Self

Technically, it is impossible to disconnect from our true self—it is our essence and always there. In other words, we cannot escape our river because it is who we are. What happens is we pinch ourselves off from the flow of our true self. The more we cut ourselves off, the less we can access our inherent wisdom. We usually create this disconnection with our thinking patterns and beliefs which then in turn motivate our action. The true self is always there and available for us to connect with at deeper levels in any given moment as we no longer continue to pull away from it. The more we connect to our true self, the less we have to practice connecting to that part of us, because we are living life more from the point of our true self and less from only our conditioned or raw self. People can connect to their true selves in different ways, and a lot of the time, particularly when we are not lost in our thoughts and emotions, the connection occurs spontaneously without any effort required. Usually when we are in the flow with something or hit our groove, we are living in the moment and from our true self. At least until we get caught up in our conditioned thoughts, emotions, and behaviors.

Ideally, we want to learn how to consciously connect to our true self and utilize the wisdom of this connection at any given moment—whenever we need it. We can consciously connect to our true self by using the True-Self Breath, something that you can practice as often as you desire. Usually, the more you practice, the better you get at it.

The True-Self Breath

- Set your intention that you wish to connect to your true self (you can do so by thinking it or speaking it out loud).
- Choose to intuitively or instinctually tune in to where your core is within your body.
- Envision a small golden sphere at your core the size of a golf ball.
- Place your hand on your body at that spot or bring your focus to that area.
- Inhale and envision your breath going through your body and into that sphere.
- Exhale and envision that same breath exiting the sphere.

Connecting to our true self may not feel hugely different. The sense of connection may be subtle, but it is there. We can connect to our true self at any time we desire. If you ever notice you are losing your connection, repeat these steps as often as you like. More often than not we want to connect to our true selves whenever we feel an unpleasant emotion or make a decision. When we have unpleasant emotions, we are usually being controlled by our conditioned egoic mind or raw self and are most likely to deal with situations in habitual ways which may not serve us. If we can connect more deeply to our true self in those moments, it will give us greater clarity about how or if to utilize that emotion for our greater benefit or to allow it to be there and live from the point of our inner truth.

Meditation

Meditation is another important way to connect with our true selves. When we sit in meditation long enough, the flow of thoughts of the conditioned egoic mind will eventually slow. In the stillness of mind, the pinching-off eases and our connection to our true self automatically grows stronger. Although definitions of meditation vary, any meditation that assists us in observing our mind and emotions or not identifying with our thoughts or emotions can increase the flow of connection to our true self. Even activities which help still the mind and can create a meditative state are useful if you find it difficult to sit still—activities like cleaning, ironing, painting, playing sport, walking, playing music, listening to music, yoga, tai chi, reading. Any activity that helps you slow down and keeps you from getting caught up in the mind or emotions can be useful.

If you find a meditation style that suits you, continue to do it. The more you meditate, the more you will automatically connect to your true self in a deeper way. You will most likely begin to develop a greater sense of peace. This is also a good time to listen to your inner voice and go beyond hearing—*feel* what it is saying.

I believe the meditation styles that help you discover and sit in the energy of your true self or provide insight into the functions of your conditioned egoic mind work best as a means to practice reconnection to your true self. Three meditation styles I personally recommend are meditative self-inquiry, mindfulness meditation, and simply resting as you witness the mind and allow it to go wherever it likes.

Meditative self-inquiry is a meditation style where you sit quietly and ask yourself the question "Who am I?" What will come up are the different ways we identify ourselves—be it our gender, a belief system we have, our personality traits, our emotional states, our body, our sensations, or even the roles that we play within our lives (mother, brother, sister, friend, worker).

The second question we can ask is: "What remains when these thoughts about ourselves change or disappear?" In the space between the thoughts and beliefs resides an inner awareness or essence that transcends external things. This is the true self—always there, watching, noticing, and waiting for us to discover and live from it. Always ready for you to access its wisdom and to enter the peace of its flow.

Mindfulness meditation is a type of meditation where you choose to place your attention onto anything that is occurring in the present moment in an open and non-judgmental way. Most commonly it is the breath, but you can choose a sound, an emotion, a thought, an activity, whatever it may be. When you become aware of your attention drifting or dragging, notice this, and gently return your attention to the original point of focus. Repeat the exercise as often as necessary. Mindfulness meditation is a useful way to utilize the information in this book. Whenever you notice any specific emotions, thoughts, beliefs, desires, urges, or behaviors, track them to the source and begin to understand how they are attempting to control an emotion. All in all, engaging in any mindful meditation is the practice of seeing through the eyes of the true self.

The third type of meditation does not really seem like a meditation in the traditional sense. It is a practice of sitting in stillness and allowing your attention to wander wherever it wants to go. If your mind gets lost in thoughts, allow it; if it focuses on the birds singing outside, allow it. Follow your mind wherever it wants to go. It may move once or one hundred times. Follow it and be aware of where it goes. Also recognize the aware part of you—the part of you doing the noticing. Eventually you will find your mind will become more still and you can sit as the awareness. Wherever your mind does go, recognize that the awareness is doing the noticing, not "you."

As a whole, I find using all three types of meditation in a combination can serve best to connect to your true self and to give you the greatest insight into your true self's communication and desires, as well as the functioning of the raw and conditioned egoic self. If you find a meditation that helps you to connect, follow the method that gives you greatest connection and insight.

Time spent meditating is a sure-fire way to create a deeper connection to your true self. I suggest adding five to ten minutes of meditation into your day as it will make a big difference in increasing the flow of your connection to you. As you do this, you will develop greater insight into how the true self relates to you and the different parts of your life-experience.

Chapter Six

The True Self's Relationship with Emotions

As you may already realize, the conditioned egoic mind is adept at attempting to control emotions. It has developed the ability over many years of learning to keep us safe from death, harm, but also emotional turmoil. It started when we were children beginning to develop an ego to assist in creating these strategies to control our feelings. When I was a child and spoke my mind about something, if it was deemed "offensive" I would receive disapproval and be told to be polite or say nothing at all. Because I did not want the pain of further disapproval, I learned to filter the things I said, which was helpful in the moment, yet through these experiences I developed sensitivity to disapproval.

We all have versions of this coping strategy. While these were useful at the time, they resulted in a blockage of emotions and a tendency for us to try to control them. So, for me it meant that whenever I experienced disapproval as an adult it was especially painful because it triggered not only current disapproval but also the unprocessed stored disapproval from my past experiences. This means we carry around a whole history of emotions within us just as a battery carries a charge of energy. When we keep attempting to control the emotions unhelpfully, this results in us still keeping the energy of those emotions stored within. When they are triggered in a current situation, the result is the whole history of that emotion being felt out in the present moment.

The innate intelligence of the true self is aware that our bodies do not wish for us to hold on to emotions. In fact, our bodies are designed to feel the emotion without any need for resistance. The true self wants us to feel the emotion so that it no longer has to be stored within us. It is our conditioned egoic mind which has learned how to resist and push the emotions down. The moment we decide to stop resisting, the emotion will arise from the depths and be felt and then released from the body. It is like holding a ball under water; the moment we stop holding it down, it will float to the surface, then float away with the current. The process of allowing the feeling assists the emotion to leave the body and no longer be stored within it. While it does not often happen overnight, it will happen more often each time we allow the emotion to be felt. The true self knows that allowing the emotion heals the body of the emotional baggage it carries due to our mind's learned control strategies. We can actually feel the emotion out of our bodies. For me, because I have learned to sit with feelings of disapproval and felt out many of the past disapproval feelings from my body, I am much less sensitive to it when it occurs.

So far, we have learned that our conditioned egoic mind's way of attempting to control our emotions, while useful at times, is eventually bound to fail, disconnect us from our true self and create further problems for us in the longer term, plus it continues to store past emotions in our bodies. But if control is all we know, then what other option do we have?

The other option we have is to listen to our true self and process emotions from its perspective. The true self is able to allow us to feel the emotions and has a peaceful, accepting relationship with the physical sensations they create within our bodies. The true self is also willing to surrender to the idea that certain emotions will arise and accepts them being a part of life. So, the best antidote to controlling or resisting emotions is to listen to the true self and allow emotions to exist, or to surrender to the idea of them existing. Stop fighting them, allow their presence, and respect their role. The true self has no interest in controlling emotions but *can* decide to control them if it seems like the right thing in the situation. By allowing them we get the option to listen to our true self and take its advice rather than blindly taking the advice of the emotion.

But how do you allow an emotion?

Before learning how to allow an emotion, it is important to understand a little bit more information about emotions and allowing them. Our conditioned egoic mind is the only part of us not allowing the emotion. Our true self will always allow it to be felt, so to follow the urge of the true self we can decide to allow emotions too.

When we think about allowing emotions, it is important to remember what emotions are. They are physiological sensations in our body designed to motivate us toward action. So, when we talk about making peace with an emotion, I am saying to make peace with the discomfort we feel in our body. The second piece of information which can help with making peace with them is allowing ourselves to feel that an emotion is not harmful to us. They cannot hurt us physically if felt; they are just uncomfortable. They can, though, be harmful if we do not allow ourselves to feel them and keep them stored in our body, which is why our true self wants them to be released.

The other thing about emotions is that if we allow them, they will always come and go independently. This is how our bodies were designed: to release emotions once they have arisen and served their purpose. It is our mind that persists in holding on to them. For our conditioned minds, the time to allow the emotion to come and go naturally is not quite quick enough, so it attempts to get rid of them as fast as possible, despite the natural ability of the true self to feel them. Emotions are also normal for us. If we feel an emotion, then based on our life lessons, beliefs, experiences, biology, brain chemistry, genetics, fatigue levels, and true self, it is normal for it to be there at that moment—

even if someone else does not feel the same thing in the same situation. Even though the emotion is normal for us, this does not mean we need to act upon it. In fact, we do not "have" to act upon emotions because they do not have to control our actions. As already mentioned, another main reason we want to make peace with emotions is because we do not have full control over them anyway, so making peace with them makes more sense to minimize our overall level of suffering as eventually we will be bound to fail at controlling them. Another reason to allow emotions is that the more we do so, the less they bother us in the long term. That is, we grow used to them, cleanse our body of them, and we no longer feel so sensitive to them when they arise. Also, in making peace with emotions they do not come as often longer term, especially with situations from the past. Further, making peace with your emotions is beneficial as the emotions are often trying to help us; they are not there to be bad to us, but rather are tools with a function. It is up to us to decide whether the tool is helping us or not. Also, allowing them will help us to release pent-up emotions from the past, thus healing us of any pain we are carrying around.

Allowing or making peace with emotions really comes down to a conscious choice to listen to the wisdom of the true self. If you practice the following exercise without the choice or decision to let all emotions exist, then it will not be beneficial. The more you hate, resist, or identify with the emotion, the stronger your suffering will be. That's why, as you practice this eight-step technique, it is important to be willing to allow emotions into your life and feel the shadow ones as fully as the light ones.

Eight Steps Toward Allowing Emotions

As you practice allowing your emotions I suggest the following eight steps. It can be useful to do these exercises with your eyes closed to focus on feeling.

1. *Be aware*: Bring your awareness to the emotion; notice where it occurs in your body and how you feel it. Notice each physical sensation.
2. *Breathe*: Breathe slowly and gently. Imagine inhaling a golden light into and around the sensations of the emotion.
3. *Space*: Picture your body like the vastness of outer space or a galaxy and imagine the emotion as one small part of the galaxy, like a star in the vastness of the sky.
4. *Let go*: Release thinking patterns attempting to control the emotion.
5. *Allow*: Allow the emotion to be there. Make the decision that you are willing to make peace with it. Make the decision to let it exist as part of your life.
6. *Respect*: Respect the emotion for trying to help and the sometimes-useful role it plays. Or practice respecting the process of the emotion ridding your body of the emotional baggage you no longer wish to store.
7. *Connect*: Connect to what advice your true self is giving you in the situation. Sense how the flow feels most aligned.
8. *Choose*: Choose to listen to your true self and decide to behave accordingly.

As you can see, allowing emotions can be a beneficial ability to utilize wisdom and develop and grow our connection to our true self. Often the willingness to let the emotion exist will result in less resistance over time (not in one go) and give us the freedom to live as our true self. Allowing emotions can also assist you in releasing past emotions that you have subconsciously stored.

Releasing Past Emotions

Just like a battery charged up with energy, we have a history of emotions stored within us, lying dormant and waiting to be triggered by some event in our lives. When the event triggers us, not only does it trigger us for that particular situation, but it also triggers the whole history of that emotion at the same time. If I was often disrespected by someone throughout my life, then feeling disrespected by anyone might trigger and unleash my whole history of being disrespected.

When we initially experienced the buildup of emotion, we were not taught or wise enough to know how to deal with it and thus coped by using whatever control strategy was available at the time. We then continued to use these control behaviors and stored up more emotion within us—sometimes to the stage where it made us sick.

To live as our true self and to not be reactive to situations, it would be useful to reduce the "charge" in this emotional battery and allow ourselves to "feel out" the emotions we have stored within our body. We can consciously do this, rather than subconsciously when it gets triggered, by connecting to emotional memories from our life. Memories from our life are thoughts or pictures in our heads of events we have experienced. Many of our unprocessed emotions have memories connected to them. In order to release these emotions it can be useful to face these memories so you can "feel out" the emotions attached to them.

Allowing ourselves to experience emotions we have been storing for so long can be problematic, though, if we decide we want to control them. That is, if we add a narrative and do not view the situation for what it was. So, again consider the example of when I received disapproval for giving my opinion. I was aware that my parents were teaching me their version of politeness out of love, but if I had a narrative that said things such as: *They should have known better...how dare they treat me like that...they were such bad parents,* this would not allow my emotion to be released but instead keep triggering and creating anger and resentment. The more cleanly we can allow ourselves to feel the emotion, the easier it will be to let it go and move on.

If I had many memories of feeling abandoned as a child, I would simply allow my mind to drift to those memories and let the emotion come up. Just allowing the emotion to be there is what is releasing it from our body.

When it comes to releasing past emotions, they may come up spontaneously during your meditation or you can consciously choose to do it for no more than five minutes a day. To do it consciously take some time out and allow your mind to drift to a memory of a time you felt whatever emotion you choose to work on. It may be helpful to start with one you feel ready to deal with and to then build up to more sensitive ones. Once the five minutes is up, show gratitude and appreciation to yourself for putting in effort to help cleanse yourself. Continue the practice until you get an intuitive sense that you no longer need to do it. This mode is a suggestion; it is important to see where you are at any given day or moment and see if you feel you are in a place where it will be helpful. If you experienced any trauma or find it too difficult to do alone, it may be useful to engage with a professional to assist.

The difference between releasing past emotions about *past* situations and feeling them for *current* situations is that most of the time we do not need to take further action regarding emotions derived from the past. They wait for us to feel them, and once felt, do not need to be addressed again. That is, unless we continue using the control narratives in an unhelpful way. This would then cause us to begin to store the emotion again and recharge that emotion's battery.

Allowing emotions helps us to release any past pain we are carrying and become less sensitive and reactive to the emotions we feel. It also provides the opportunity to connect to our true self and follow our heart's desires instead of the habitual behavioral patterns we are taught. Another way to do this is by growing our capacity for self-love.

Chapter Seven

Self-Love

When it comes to listening to our true self, it is useful to know how it speaks to us and what strategies we can practice to grow better attuned with what it has to say. The best label I've found to describe the true self's communication is "self-love." But what is self-love? It is definitely a term that gets thrown around a lot, but no one ever really tells us what it is or how to do it. Self-love is a combination of internal thinking patterns and external behaviors toward ourselves, others, and the world that encompass how we think, talk, relate, and act. Even though the natural state of our true self is a loving one, many of us have learned to be hard on ourselves and not look after ourselves in a kind or loving way. We might be taught to offer these things externally but not enough of them internally. Perhaps we even treat others with the harshness we treat ourselves with.

In general, if these internal or external behaviors make us feel worse about ourselves or another, then they are not likely to be self-loving and are not the communication of the true self. Contrarily, if they do make us feel even a bit better about ourselves, they are most likely self-loving and coming from the place more closely aligned to the true self. Self-loving is our natural state; it is through our life-experiences and how we were treated by those around us that we learn how to treat ourselves differently from our natural state. If those around us showed love in a critical, hard, or harsh way, we are more likely to treat ourselves similarly. If we were gently nurtured, with more love and encouragement, we more than likely have better ways of loving ourselves.

Following are behaviors which I feel constitute self-love and most closely represent how the true self treats us. They may seem natural to you or quite foreign. Engaging in self-loving behaviors is a choice we have at any given moment. If we have not learned to do them then this choice may seem difficult. The more you choose it and the more often you do them, the easier it will be to cope with and also soften the edges of whatever emotions you may be feeling when they arise. Plus, it will also help you in creating an internal content and dialogue derived less from the outside world and more in alignment with the real you.

Self-Care

Care toward others comes naturally for most of us. When we see someone else in pain, we have enough empathy to know how they might feel and then offer them some level of care. Doing this for ourselves tends not to be as easy. Being self-caring usually involves doing things for ourselves to look after ourselves or treat ourselves well. They could be things we enjoy or things that make us feel good or healthier. It could also be allowing ourselves to do nothing at all or asking for help. Self-caring can take different forms but can fall under categories such as looking after our health, doing things for fun, choosing activities that help us relax, exercising, eating well, nourishing our body, practicing good sleep hygiene, pampering ourselves.

When deciding on how to be self-caring, it can be helpful to ask: *What would I do for someone I cared about if they were in the situation I was in?* Once you have your answer, see if you can turn that behavior onto yourself. You may also like to take some time to ask yourself: *What activities make me feel better and help me care for myself?* Once you have done this, set some small achievable goals of when you would like to do those self-caring activities.

Make the decision to love yourself enough to care about you. Self-caring is a useful tool when feeling any emotion.

Self-Compassion/Compassion

Compassion when given to others is defined as a deep level of concern about another for their suffering or emotional turmoil. When turned in on ourselves, we offer the same level of concern and kindness to ourselves. Self-compassion is similar to self-caring, but it is more about how we care about ourselves internally with our beliefs and attitudes toward ourselves—having a kinder and softer relationship within. We can recognize that sometimes being a human is tough and we are going to struggle and not live up to our expectations. We are going to make mistakes and not always get everything "right." It is the recognition that we have all had different life-experiences, different beliefs, different emotional sensitivities, and different reactions to our lives.

Offering ourselves compassion and fairness is giving ourselves permission to be an imperfect human and being fair on ourselves in the times where we are suffering the most or do not like what we see in ourselves. To do so we can learn to speak to ourselves with understanding, fairness, and kindness as if we were talking to the person we loved the most in the whole world in a moment of their deepest pain, or perhaps like talking to the 5-year-old version of yourself who is struggling to understand the world and is trying to cope the best they can. Turning this form of self-love onto ourselves can assist us in normalizing our pain and allowing ourselves to be imperfect people who are trying our best with what we have and growing with every attempt. Self-compassion can be really useful with any of the emotions.

Compassion for others can be extremely useful to us also, because when we have a level of compassion for others it minimizes the anger and hate we have in our bodies. Others, like us, are trying the best they can with what they have. Compassion for others can be useful when you feel sad, disappointed, guilty, lonely, hurt, rejected, abandoned, unworthy, or any of the anger emotions.

To do any version of compassion it would be useful to find some lighter thoughts in relation to yourself or others. Create thoughts that are kinder, softer, and fairer to you or them. Thoughts that highlight that it is okay to struggle at times, to not be perfect, that you are in a process of growth and you are okay to just be you.

Self-Respect

To have respect is to have regard for a person and their wishes, wants, and rights. It is to take into consideration what it is they feel and to treat them in a way that acknowledges their right to be alive. Respecting another is treating or speaking to them as an equal and giving them the same rights you yourself would like to have. Most of us will have different definitions about what levels of respect we can agree on, but when turning it on ourselves it is mostly about how we speak to ourselves and what behaviors we engage in. Speaking to ourselves and treating our body in a kind, nice, gentle way which builds us up rather than tears us down is considered being self-respecting. Behaving in ways that give us access to the rights we want as a human also represents a self-respecting behavior. Giving self-respect is always important but can be extremely useful when you have feelings of disappointment, guilt, loneliness, rejection, abandonment, low self-worth, or any of the self-hate emotions.

A good practice for self-respect is to close your eyes and imagine you are standing in front of the person you respect most in the world. Then ask yourself: *What would I ideally say or do to them to give them the most respect possible?* Then decide to turn this onto yourself.

Self-Encouragement

Encouraging is the act of giving someone support, hope, or confidence to forge ahead. It logically follows that self-encouragement is the ability to do those things for ourselves. Encouraging ourselves is the act of helping to propel ourselves forward in a difficult situation despite the unpleasant feelings we may be experiencing. Many of us get stuck in the unfairness or the pain of the situation and use words or perceptions which keep us stuck in a spiral of suffering and do not assist us to move past or through what is going on for us. Knowing how to use motivating words which assist us in working through the situation and then acting upon those words will definitely minimize any time we may spend in the specific emotional states. Self-encouragement is a useful self-love tool to use when you feel stuck in any emotional state.

An example of a self-encouraging question to ask yourself is: *I feel [name the emotion], but how do I want to move forward despite feeling this way?* Or perhaps: *What is one small step I can take to move forward right now?* Repeat the question once you have completed that step, and so on.

Forgiveness and Self-Forgiveness

Forgiveness is a conscious decision to stop holding on to anger, hate, and resentment toward oneself or another person. It is the willingness to let ourselves or the other person off the hook for what it is they have done in order to be free of the pain we are carrying toward them or ourselves. Ultimately all forgiveness, whether for self or others, is of benefit to us, and thus an act of self-loving. Most of us have a tough time trying to forgive another person or ourselves as the propulsion of anger and hate makes us feel powerful toward the other and thus decreases our feelings of pain temporarily. Other times, we think we or the other person does not deserve to be forgiven so we hold on to the anger as a form of punishing ourselves or the other. We can also refuse to forgive out of fear that if we let ourselves or the other off the hook, we or they will once again hurt us or cause us more pain. By holding on we are already guaranteeing pain. To hold on to the anger or hate, we must keep it in our body, and thus in not forgiving we are only hurting ourselves.

Forgiving benefits us. It relieves us of feelings of anger, hate, or resentment and leaves us feeling less burdened and more self-loved. The willingness to forgive yourself or others will truly set you free. Forgiveness does not mean you must forget what happened and keep the person in your life (unless it is yourself you are forgiving). It is best used with the emotions of guilt, disappointment, hurt, rejection, anger, self-hate, and abandonment.

An exercise to develop your ability to forgive yourself or others is to sit quietly and put your hand on your heart. Once you have done this, imagine your heart filling with a pink light of forgiveness. As it begins to grow full, say to yourself: "I forgive myself/them for..." and state what that is. For example, "I forgive myself for my mistakes," "I forgive myself for being imperfect," "I forgive them for hurting me." You may experience some resistance. If this is the case, change the wording to make it lighter and more in line with where you are in the process, such as "I would like to be able to forgive myself/them for..."

Appreciation and Self-Appreciation

To appreciate is to recognize the full worth of someone or something. When turned upon ourselves, it is obviously to recognize and celebrate the full worth of ourselves. When turned outward, it is about appreciating the good in our life.

Appreciating ourselves and our life and the good we have in it can lead us to feel more content and happier with what we have. Appreciation is about focusing on the good aspects of what we have and ignoring some of the "negative" aspects about ourselves or our life. We are taught from a young age to appreciate the others around us, but many of us have not been taught how to appreciate ourselves. In fact, sometimes when we did appreciate ourselves we were told we were being too big-headed or conceited so we were left feeling guilty or ashamed that we had appreciated or liked ourselves even for a moment. From then on, we became harder on ourselves and only focused on our weaknesses, which often left us feeling not good enough. We all have strengths and weaknesses; appreciating our strengths does not negate a weakness, nor does focusing on a weakness negate a strength.

An exercise to grow your ability to self-appreciate is by creating a list of things you are good at, things you like about yourself, improvements you have made or barriers you have overcome. Remember this list especially when feeling the emotions of disappointment, guilt, loneliness, hurt, rejection, abandonment, and unworthiness.

We have also been taught to focus on problems, so that we can look at them and possibly be able to solve them. When we are attuned to problems, we often never take time to look at the good we have. Life will always involve good and bad; appreciating the good, despite the problems or bad that exists, is paramount in assisting us to feel better despite some of the pain we can experience.

An exercise in appreciation can involve creating a list of the things you appreciate which are either good or neutral from your past and present life. It can also be useful at the end of every day to see if you can find at least three things you can appreciate about your day. Self-appreciation and appreciation can help us connect more deeply to our true self when we are feeling sad, unworthy, dissatisfied, hopeless, directionless, hurt, empty, or powerless.

Self-Acceptance

To accept means to fully embrace something exactly as it is without it requiring change. Self-accepting is our natural state. We are not born in resistance to ourselves. Most of us today, though, will struggle to accept many things about ourselves we do not like and will therefore resort to hate or anger to cope with our disdain for those things. We have learned we must look or behave a certain way to be accepted. Because of this, when we did not follow or have what was deemed acceptable, we received rejection from others. From the rejection, we then learned to self-reject those qualities or behaviors we learned were bad, wrong, or undesirable within ourselves.

The truth is we all have qualities which are undesirable at times and desirable at other times. Only accepting ourselves when we display them and rejecting ourselves when we do not will only cause us shame and self-hatred and force us to hide away anything we believe is bad. Everyone has every quality available to humans and there is no right or wrong amount of those qualities to have. Plus, every quality we possess can assist us at any given moment. Self-acceptance means acknowledging and not rejecting yourself—all your qualities, thoughts, emotions, urges, physicality, gender, sexuality. It is to accept every little part of you, no matter how good or bad you or others view it.

Are you willing to accept yourself with the qualities you possess, whether or not you learned they were bad or good? Self-acceptance is useful at any time, but particularly when feeling disappointed, guilty, lonely, hurt, rejected, abandoned, unworthy, and when experiencing self-hate.

Practice self-acceptance by choosing a part of yourself you notice yourself rejecting. List as many benefits or uses you can think of for this part and then choose some lighter thoughts to describe it. For example, disliking your selfishness could look like: *it is wrong to be selfish; I'm a bad person for being so selfish; others' needs are more important than mine.* Lighter thoughts could look like: *it is okay to be selfish sometimes; everyone has selfishness in them; selfishness is another word for being self-giving; it is important to give to yourself; selfishness helps me get my needs met; without it I would have nothing; it can help me to not be taken advantage of.* Pay attention to how much you resist or accept the thoughts, and grow the self-acceptance and lightness of thought from there.

Self-Advocating

Advocating for oneself is about learning when it feels right and true to speak up and stand up for what is important to you. It may require you to step outside of your comfort zone and say the things that are on your mind. It may require you to set a boundary or limits with another person; it may require you to communicate exactly how you feel about a situation. If you are someone who over-advocates, it may also require you to speak a little less, in a kinder way, more gently, or not at all. Either way, it is about you being willing to speak and act in a way that supports your truest interests without belittling or negating the value of the other person. It means using your voice to speak in an aligned, helpful, and respectful way to get your message across for your truest benefit.

Ask yourself some of these questions regarding self-advocating:

If I were not scared to talk, what would I like to say?
If I truly believed I was important enough to have my needs met, what would I like to ask for?

If someone asks me for something, how would I like to hear it?
What feels like the most aligned way to advocate for myself?

Surrender and Acceptance

Our true self knows when it could be useful for us to control things and when it would be useful to surrender to whatever may be or accept whatever is or was. Our egoic mind does not, and this leads us to further pain and suffering. The true self accepts everything in you and your life as it is right now; it also accepts everything going on in the world right now, and everything which has ever occurred. Your true self accepts every single person exactly as they are. It has no need to change anything or anyone. However, it is capable of changing things should that change feel right to you. By practicing acceptance, you are practicing listening to your true self and bringing about the peace that comes with it. The best way to practice acceptance is to make peace with and allow whatever emotion is arising and to choose lighter thoughts about how you perceive it.

Surrender is about letting go of the need to control the current flow of life and where it may lead in the future. Our true self exists only in this moment and is in flow with life how it is without having to control, know or prepare for the future. Are you willing to listen to your true self and surrender your need to control the flow of life and what it may bring and allow yourself to experience the peace that comes with it?

To improve your ability to surrender, it is valuable to practice accepting emotions (in particular fear) as this will give you more confidence in yourself to manage whatever emotion may arise in the situation you fear losing control of. To discover the other emotion you could make peace with, ask yourself: "What am I scared I will feel if I let go in this situation?" Practicing surrender with self-trust will also help.

Self-Trust

To trust is to have a firm belief in the reliability or truth of something or someone. Ultimately all trust is self-trust. Most of us consider trusting others or the world as taking a leap of faith because we may not be certain the person is trustworthy. In actuality, to trust another we must first trust ourselves enough to believe that what we feel about them is correct. We must first have faith in ourselves and our judgment if we are to trust another person.

Many people do not have trust in themselves because they have become jaded by the outcomes of their past decisions or relied on others to make their decisions for them. This causes them to be plagued by doubt and uncertainty—which, while having the ability to assist our lives at times, can also leave us feeling paralyzed within our choices. To trust yourself is to do what feels right and take a leap of faith in yourself and your judgment and abilities. We need self-trust for any decision we make in our lives, and like trust for others, we can grow it with the positive reinforcement of the outcomes we get. It is also a lot easier to trust yourself when you know how to manage any emotions that may arise, as there is nothing left to fear if you are able to navigate the emotional consequences. Self-trust is especially useful with the anxiety emotions and can also be applied to your ability to manage the emotions outlined in this book.

Difficulties with self-trust often create anxiety within us. So as to not overly trigger anxiety and instead to grow your self-trust, it will be beneficial for you to go slowly. Try this exercise: think of a small area in your life where you doubt yourself. Perhaps it's *doubting your ability to drive to a new place.* From there, surrender to the idea of making a wrong decision or looking stupid. So it might be *surrendering to the idea of getting lost and people judging you.* Once you have done that, decide you are going to take a chance on yourself and stick with the decision that feels most aligned to your true self in the situation. So, it might look like *driving to the destination and stopping as many times as needed*. Be willing to do this repeatedly, even if it doesn't go well at first. As you become more adept at trusting yourself in smaller parts of your life, move on to the bigger ones.

Courage/Bravery

To have courage is to have the ability to do something we feel scared to do. We all have a sense of bravery to us. We have done things we were scared to do, and many of those times our bravery has paid off and we no longer have that fear to do those things. Even if we do feel scared, we have a sense of pride in facing the fear at that time. Having bravery is an important part of living life. Bravery is not doing something in the absence of fear, but more a case of doing it because it is of importance to us, even though we experience fear. We are going to face new things in our lives, and we also worry about facing old things which have haunted us. It takes bravery and courage to decide to love ourselves enough to live a rich, meaningful life, the one our true self wills for us.

If you experience fear, ask yourself if you are willing to be brave enough to do what is important to you even if the outcome could be emotional or physical pain. When you do this repeatedly, your bravery will increase and your fear decrease. Bravery is a useful tool when you feel the anxiety emotions.

Just like self-trust, bravery grows best at a slow pace so it is easier to cultivate within yourself. Choose a small goal you are willing to be brave enough to face which is aligned with your true self. Surrender to whatever the outcome may be and trust yourself to manage the emotion; if not, be willing to learn from it. Choose small meaningful steps and slowly grow them to greater and more meaningful goals to you.

***

As you may have discovered while reading this chapter, the ability to love yourself and practice these self-love skills is not always easy. You may find some come more easily, while you may have a lot of resistance to others—even to the thought of them! This is normal and most likely means you never learned those areas of self-love. So, our goal from here is to cultivate and nurture our ability to self-love and listen to our true self. The more you are willing to practice these behaviors, the more your connection to true self will increase. The more your self-love increases, the easier it will be to deal with any emotional pain you may be feeling. It starts with a willingness, a desire, and a choice to build self-love within. If you do not make the conscious choice, you will still be able to access self-love, but it will likely involve more emotional pain before you reach that point of connection. It helps to do so slowly and to begin by changing your perceptions to make them lighter instead of heavier or darker.

While we may never have really learned self-love as I have described it, our conditioned mind has nonetheless developed strategies to create some version of self-love. It has developed thinking and behavior tools to help us minimize our pain, which at times can be self-loving, but when overused or utilized in an unaligned way creates much suffering. That's why our next goal is to understand these strategies in order to use them in a more self-loving way aligned with our true self.

SECTION 3

Tools of the Conditioned Egoic Mind

Chapter Eight

What Is the Conditioned Egoic Mind?

I'm really good at flying under the radar. It is not something I try to do; it just feels normal because I have been doing it for so long. I am the kind of person who can live in a place for many years and yet people will still think I am a newcomer when they meet me. This avoidance strategy of flying under the radar was something I developed as a child and teenager. Through some of my experiences, my mind developed strategies to keep me emotionally safer in the environments I was in.

The part of our mind that works to try to minimize our emotional pain in an attempt to love ourselves is what I call the conditioned egoic mind. Through lessons and conditioning of our lives and the responses and memories, we have developed an ego. The ego is the part of our mind that identifies with us as a "self" attached to our body, our thoughts, and our emotions. The conditioned egoic mind attempts to help keep us alive and cared for by creating an identity we say is a "me." It tries to get this "me" to feel pleasant or familiar as much as possible as a way of loving it. It holds on to a lot of fear about the death of the "me" and it will do anything it can to sustain the momentum of the self, as it fears if it were to not exist, we would die. So, to do this our mind learns to control things, whether it be ourselves, other people, situations, and especially our emotions. It attempts to help the "me" avoid and solve unpleasant emotions and to chase the pleasant ones within us. It will also attempt to keep the "me" in a familiar emotional state as a means of safety, whether it is pleasant or not. It does these things in an attempt to be "self-loving."

To do this it developed emotional thoughts and resistance behaviors. We learned these behaviors out of necessity—to cope with our emotions and to stay alive. We learned them from the people around us (mostly primary caregivers) and by watching and observing other people's reactions to their emotions, as well as their reactions to us and the world. We also learn by trial and error. Unconsciously identifying with aspects of "self" and then engaging in the emotional thoughts and resistance behaviors of the conditioned egoic mind is what can most disconnect us from our true self as we get lost in habitual patterns of thinking or action. Control/resistance behaviors can be defined as anything we do either internally (conditioned egoic thinking) or externally (resistance behaviours) to reduce, solve, avoid, or change our emotions.

Many of these behaviors have been successful in helping us love ourselves enough to feel better, stay alive, make our lives easier, and thus be able to live as our true selves. They can help us fix things and improve situations to make them less problematic and more peaceful for us. They can enhance our likelihood of survival and make sure our needs are met. They can help us change what we are doing and adapt to situations so that we get the most desired outcome. In other words, the conditioned egoic mind is not all bad. It offers tools that can help us function and feel better—just as, by learning to fly under the radar, my mind kept me out of sight because "being out of sight" mostly meant being emotionally safer.

When used to extreme or excess, especially unconsciously, these tools keep us enslaved in behaviors which do not always serve us to live as our true selves. Even though a particular behavior might offer us some short-term reprieve of our shadow emotions, it can also have the ability to enhance our suffering and pain in the longer term. Becoming enslaved by these behaviors can disconnect us from our true self and thus leave us feeling unfulfilled and unaware of what it is we truly want in a situation. These behaviors tend not to be flexible and often result in our mind attempting to use the same behaviors (whether useful or not useful) repeatedly to deal with our emotions and situations. So, me always flying under the radar means I am safe, but I also miss out on building meaningful relationships if I keep doing it.

What the egoic mind is not aware of is that even if it were to die, we would still exist. The fraudulent identities of self might go, but we exist without the need to identify with thoughts or emotions. Our true self exists far beyond our mind or emotional states. Plus, our job is not to kill the conditioned egoic mind, but to learn how to utilize it as a tool for our true self to live a self-loving, rich, meaningful, and content life aligned with our natural flow without overly identifying with it as ourselves.

The behaviors in which we partake to keep the self alive, feeling good, and secure can be both internal and external processes we have learned through our experiences. They can help us live a safe and good life, or they can imprison us and make our lives hell. The main issue overall with any conditioned egoic thoughts or behaviors is that while they can be useful, eventually they are bound to fail, as we do not have full control over our situations, or our emotions, and they are not flexible enough to assist us in living our truest lives. The best way to know if the egoic mind assists us is to consider if what it is saying aligns with the urge of the true self.

Chapter Nine

The Call of the True Self and Aligned Action

Just like a river's current might gently draw us into its flow, the true self will gently draw us toward the flow of life, which is our own natural course. We do not need to listen; our conditioned egoic mind will pull us in the other direction toward behaviors that assist us in controlling emotions, and we can choose to follow it if we wish. However, these behaviors do not always go along with the calling of the true self, aligned action. When sitting solely as our true selves without resisting its gentle pull, which communicates through instinct, intuitive thoughts, and emotions, we will just be the observer of them. Buddhists call this the "backward step," and if it is the backward step, then the egoic mind wants us to always take a "forward step." Living in the forward step keeps us a slave to our egoic mind, while living solely in the backward step can create a complete disconnection from our thoughts and feelings and we can easily get lost in a desire to avoid life altogether and experience it from this detached vantage point. While perhaps we would not identify with our experience or pains, we would also be depriving ourselves of a meaningful existence. To engage in aligned action requires us to surrender to the urge of the true self within any given situation, then take an aligned forward step. Choosing to surrender to the call of our true self means getting to know ourselves and deciding at any given moment what feels true to us in a situation—despite how we may feel emotionally—and engaging in that behavior.

When we do not need to decide about taking action, it can be far easier to live according to our truths. For example, if you are watching TV or just driving from one place to the next, there is no need for thinking or emotional reactions involved. It is easy to enact the calling of the true self and take the aligned forward step. During an emotionally charged situation, things may get difficult when we feel emotions and must decide on a course of action. To make the truest choice in relation to actions it is important for us to understand ourselves and to tune in to our heart's deepest desires, what is true to us, and to base our choice of action on what aligns with the true self's urge.

To do so we must first take a step back and notice and understand our habitual responses to our emotions so we can consciously make a choice that is most aligned with our inner truth. To be able to take this step back requires us to sit as the awareness of the true self, accept the emotions and the conditioned strategies we have to control them, accept the situation and/or surrender to a situation before attempting to control it with the aligned forward step. This backward step frees us from control by our egoic thoughts and behavioral reactions, enabling us to instead decide from a deeper place of truth about what aligned forward step would best serve the current situation (which can involve following the egoic mind too). To do so, it would serve us to learn about the skills and behaviors our mind has developed to control emotions.

When you sit in a mindful meditation or the meditation where you allow your attention to wander, you are actually practicing taking the backward step. You are there training yourself to notice your innate and egoic emotions and your egoic thoughts without getting caught up in the action of them. The goal from here is to be able to bring this practice into real-world experience, not only the meditation chair. You do this by cultivating your awareness of your conditioned egoic behaviors and their triggers. So, it is important to realize what egoic behaviors you have. As they follow beliefs and emotions, it is helpful to ask: *What beliefs and emotions occur before this behavior?*

Chapter Ten

Conditioned Egoic Thoughts

My mind is a natural problem solver. I'm not saying that I am always good at solving problems, but I'm always good at spotting them and coming up with possible solutions to a problem. For me, the process occurs automatically. It may have started out as innate to me but has definitely been reinforced by my experiences—by my life of seeing a situation and finding a solution for the best way to navigate through the situation with the least amount of emotional turmoil. This is how our conditioned egoic thoughts work.

Conditioned egoic thoughts are thinking patterns, choices, and attitudes we hold that we utilize to deal with emotions and situations when they arise. There are numerous types of these thoughts and many of them are connected to specific feelings. They always come secondary to our beliefs and emotional states, and when they do not assist, they not only intensify our resistance to the primary emotion but also create resistance emotions, leading to further suffering. So, knowing what our mind will say and when or if to use these conditioned egoic thoughts to assist us in living our truest life is of utmost importance for a life of peace.

Following are descriptions of many conditioned egoic thinking patterns we hold as humans and the uses and pitfalls that can arise when utilizing them or overusing them.

Identifying with Thoughts or Labels

Our conditioned egoic self is something that only exists in our minds. It is a bunch of beliefs we have learned to identify with as ourselves. These thoughts usually start with the words *I am* and can be followed by a whole array of labels which supposedly represent who we are. *I am smart/dumb. I am a father/mother. I am a perfectionist. I am left/right leaning. I am a specific gender. I am a certain sexual orientation. I am a worrier. I am a people pleaser. I am a hard worker. I am a victim. I am selfish/giving. I am a Christian/Buddhist/Muslim. I am the job I do.* The list could go on and on. We think what we say about ourselves is who we are. If told anything different we get fearful and angry and want to defend ourselves because it feels like we are losing our identities.

These labels are not all bad. They can help us identify within us certain leanings and orientations that feel most true to us. They can help us create definitions of what they mean, which can help lead to doing certain behaviors which may serve us. As an example, me identifying as a psychologist or spiritual teacher could help me follow the ethical guidelines that might come with that label. Or, identifying as a mother could help you be the type of mother you truly want to be.

Problems arise when we think we are the label itself, rather than the person the label is placed upon. I act as and am labeled "psychologist or spiritual teacher," but it is not who I am. I am me always, but not these things at every given moment. We are not always going to be in the role, and when we lose it, we will feel like we have lost ourselves. But I am as I am, no matter what label is put on me by others or my egoic self. Another issue with the labels is that identifying with them as who we are locks us into behaving as versions of those things we have learned. If I believe I am a victim, I am going to behave like a victim. If I believe I am self-sacrificing, I engage in self-sacrificing behaviors and thoughts so as not to lose my identity.

If identifying to some degree with a thought can serve you and make your life better, continue using it. If you find you are identifying solely as those beliefs or labels, it would be useful to drop it as your identity and remember that you are already who you are. Arriving at your place of true self will help you decide upon or act out the best behavior in any situation.

Identifying with Emotions

Just like we identify with thoughts as ourselves, we also can have a tendency to identify with ourselves as whatever emotional state we are currently experiencing or have experienced regularly or in the past. We might say: *I am a happy person, I am an anxious person, I am angry, I am hurt, I am disappointed, I am a depressed person.* In a sense we think we are what we feel. We do not recognize that we are the ones feeling these emotions; we are not the emotion itself. We are aware of the emotions arising, but we are also the ones aware of the emotions disappearing. We exist even when those emotions are not there, so we cannot possibly be the emotion itself. The emotions always come and go, yet our true self still remains.

There are two main issues which occur when we overly identify with ourselves as our emotions. The first is: the more we identify with our emotional state, the more we create the emotion within us. If I believe I am an anxious person, I am subconsciously willing myself to feel more anxious as I have created my identity around it. The same goes for the other emotions. The other issue arising from identifying with emotions is: we feel we must act on them whenever they occur within us. Always acting on emotions can be problematic and lead us further out of alignment with the true self.

Being aware of the emotions and identifying with them occurring within us, though, can be helpful at times. Having awareness can help us decide if the emotion is a useful one to listen to and to act upon. The emotion may be trying to communicate a message to us from our true self. As I've mentioned, emotions can function as an internal compass to help our true self find a way forward, an action, or a solution within a situation.

If identifying with the emotion helps you to act or behave in a certain way which feels true to you, great! Utilize the identification and take its advice. If it is not expressing your true needs, allow it to be there without identifying yourself as it. Remember, you are you all the time; your emotions come and go, but you always remain.

Apart from identifying with emotions and thoughts, our conditioned egoic mind also has many thinking strategies to assist us in coping with the world we live in. In the following sections, we look at many of the main ones we use and their purposes and limitations.

Fault Finding and Problem Solving

The human mind is adept at finding faults and problems. In fact, our whole development and evolution as a species depended on this ability. Spotting a problem prompts us to go into problem-solving mode and fix it. If we were cold and it was a problem, it led us to utilizing fire or clothing as a solution. Our ability to see and solve a problem was what helped us not only survive but also thrive as a species. It assists us with our everyday life, seeing what is not working well and finding ways to make it better.

While useful at times, it is this ability to see fault in situations that will keep us unhappy, dissatisfied, and feeling not good enough. A standard of perfection rarely exists, which means that at any given moment we will be able to focus on a fault or a problem. Three main issues occur with this type of thinking pattern. The first is that we will never feel satisfied when we always focus on problems, because they will never end. Even if we were to fix the fault that we were aware of, our mind, being the fault finder and problem solver it is, will just move on to the next issue "needing" solving for us to be at peace.

The next issue is that finding fault and being problem-focused when a situation is out of your control will leave you sad, frustrated, and powerless. The more your mind then keeps focusing on it, the worse you will continue to feel.

The third issue with this type of thinking pattern arises because it is a skewed way of seeing the world. When our mind only sees problems, it ignores and takes for granted all the good. It focuses on the gaps but ignores the completeness of life exactly how it is, and takes the good for granted, leaving us forever feeling dissatisfied.

If fault finding and problem solving are helping you with your current situation, great! Keep on using that tool for your benefit. If, however, you find that you are very often problem-focused, cannot solve the fault, or you are skewed in your view of your life, then it would serve you to let go of those thoughts as often as possible and practice focusing on appreciation of the life you have and the completeness in your current situation, not what your mind views as missing.

Worry

Worry is our mind's attempt to control and seize power. It is something we all do. It is a style of thinking where our minds project into the future to preempt possible outcomes. Worry is a type of emotional thinking that stems from feelings within the uncertainty, vulnerability and fear emotions. We only worry when we feel uncertain, scared or vulnerable about something. Worry can assist the true self by helping us to prepare for what may be to come in order for us to prevent a "bad outcome." For example, worrying about dying from smoking can help us decide to quit; worrying about missing a mortgage repayment can help us save money or set it aside. Worry can also help us assess certain risks for the future and help us decide if it is necessary to take the risk at all; for example, worrying about the dangers of going on a trip or driving a car can help us decide if it is worth doing. Worry can also assist in creating a backup plan in case things go wrong, just like a savings account might be insurance against losing your job. Worry can be a useful tool to call us to action when we need to make our lives easier and eliminate or prevent emotional and physical pain.

Worry, when overused, can also cause major problems. It has the tendency to make us feel anxious and can even lead to depression. Worry often has a negative impact on us when it does not help in solving or minimizing our uncertainty or vulnerability levels. This will occur when we worry about something we have no ability to prevent or prepare for, such as worrying about my aeroplane crashing while I'm on it, or worrying about your child getting hurt when they are away from home. Worry can also be problematic when we are indecisive about what to do. If we do not make a choice to take a risk or not take it, worry can keep us paralyzed and we will never do anything. For example, you may not like your current job, but you're worried to leave in case you do not like the potential new job. So, you stay where you are and become more unhappy. Worry, once having already decided on engaging in an action, can also be problematic as it can make your overall levels of anxiety higher while you partake in the activity. For example, you have decided to leave the job, but now you are still worrying whether you are going to like the new one. Or perhaps you have created the Plan B, but you continue to worry about what is going to happen. For example, you have planned an outdoor party and have decided if it rains you will have the party at your home. Worrying beyond this will cause us anxiety and cause the week or weeks leading up to the party to be stressful. Another issue with worry arises when we can prevent the situation from occurring through our actions, but the prevention comes at too high a cost. For example, if I were to guarantee avoidance of rejection, I would never talk to anyone and quite probably feel lonely. The high cost usually ends up involving more suffering and emotional pain.

If worry does help you live from the point of your true self by minimizing uncertainty and vulnerability (through preparing, planning, or preventing a bad outcome), great! Continue to use it. But if worry does not help you control the situation and prepare, or has already outlived its use in the situation, then it would be best to thank that part of your mind for trying to help through worry, but its help is not required this time and is only making you feel worse and suffer more. Find some lighter thoughts to address the situation instead.

Common types of worried conditioned thoughts:

- What if? *What if the house burns down? What if I get hurt? What if it is the wrong decision? What if I fail?*
- Predictions. *The house will burn down. We are going to be late. I am going to fail.*
- Mind reading. *She's going to think I'm crazy. Those people won't like me. They will think that I'm weird.*
- Might, maybe, or could... *He might reject me. I could lose my job. Maybe someone is trying to break into our house.*
- *It's not worth trying.*

Common resistance behaviors that accompany worry are:

- Avoidance
- Procrastination
- Indecision
- Compulsive behaviors: hand washing, hoarding
- Double checking
- Safety behaviors (anything you do "just in case")
- Perfectionist behaviors

Dwelling and Ruminating

Dwelling or ruminating is the process by which our mind reminds us of an issue, problem, or fear. It differs from worry in that rumination usually dwells on things from the past or present, not the future. Our mind continues to think about what has happened or what is happening to remind us there is an unpleasant emotional situation going on for us that our conditioned egoic mind feels must be solved. It might look like dwelling on money problems, or continually thinking about how much you would like a relationship or how much you hate your job or how your parents treated you as a child.

Dwelling can be of assistance to us by not allowing us to forget something of importance. By being continually reminded of the issue, our mind is ensuring that we pay enough attention to the situation to solve the issue in order to help us feel emotionally pleasant or let go of or learn from the past, so we do not repeat what has been done. For example, thinking about a job that makes you feel sad could help you decide to leave the job. If we did not stop to reflect about the important things in our lives, we would have no impetus to change these situations. We would also have no desire to stop and learn from the past and would therefore keep repeating the same behaviors. For example, thinking about how I stuffed up in a presentation can help me look at the ways to do it better the next time. Ruminating also makes us feel as though we have control within the situation in some way and we are being constructive in solving it.

Problems with dwelling/ruminating can occur in numerous ways. One such way is when we cannot solve the issue we constantly think about, or the solution is not available to us right now. The rumination in these situations can lead to us feeling *more* of the emotion that the dwelling is trying to solve. For example, constantly thinking about how much you hate your job when you are not in a position to leave will reinforce the sadness you feel about the job. Dwelling is also a major issue when we continue to ruminate upon things that happened in the past and cannot be changed. We hold on to hurt or anger someone has caused us and persist in thinking about what they did. When it comes to learning from the past, dwelling can also be problematic when we attempt to teach ourselves in a self-critical way. Instead of learning in a way that moves us forward, we keep ruminating upon how bad we were, or how dumb, or what we should have done instead. This type of ruminating creates more suffering, keeps us stuck in the past, and stops us from moving forward.

If ruminating or dwelling about a situation helps you solve a problem or learn from it, then use those thoughts to help you to move forward. If you are dwelling on a past or current situation which cannot be changed (or changed right now), it may be useful to thank your mind for reminding you about the issue but remember that it is okay to feel the emotion about what is going on, without having to solve it. Also, if this rumination is self-critical, you can decide to take the lessons which are important, talk to yourself in a kind, self-loving way, and remind your egoic mind that you have learned your lesson and don't need any further reminders.

Dwelling/rumination-type thoughts are those we use to control our emotions by going over and over the issue. Any type of thinking pattern can turn into dwelling when we stay stuck in it.

Should/Should Not

We live and view life from an internal standard that we expect ourselves, people, and the world around us to meet. The internal standard often takes the form of the thinking pattern of "should" or "should not." That is, we have these internal "rules" of how we should/should not behave or be or how the world should/should not be. It is with these "shoulds" that we try to make sense of the world and use them to motivate us to behave in a desirable way. Having this "should" can be a way to help us move toward a target or desired outcome and also avoid an undesired outcome.

Beneficially speaking, "should" can help us look at what we do not like and find ways to change it for the better. Being aware of an outcome or behavior that is undesirable and then being aware of the desired ones can give us a direction and goal to work toward designed to give us a sense of fulfillment when it is achieved. For example, "There should be no war." This "should" can be useful to give us a direction and steps to help us work upon moving toward a world where no war exists and thus having the fulfillment of peace. Having a "should" can also help us understand that there can be another way to how things are. Knowing the other way is a form of problem solving and goal setting to work upon creating the reality of the other way. The other purpose for "should" is to assist us in setting limits with people for how we would like them to treat us. We can let them know what it is we want from them and what it is we do not want, or advocate for the treatment we desire. For example, *The boss should not be treating me like that; I'm going to talk to HR*. "Shoulds" can also assist us in motivating our behavior toward an outcome that makes us feel better and avoids an unpleasant emotion, such as: *I should exercise if I want to get fit*. Should-type thoughts can also be useful ways to convince others to think about a situation in the same way we do and to get them to believe our way is the better way.

"Shoulds," though, can be extremely problematic for us in numerous ways. One reason is that these standards we have are not shared among all people. That is, everyone has a different idea of what should or should not occur. This can create much external conflict, not to mention inner conflict when the "should" is not met. Another problem with "shoulds" is that they can be extremely idealistic. The expectation is too high or unrealistic when compared to the reality of the situation. For example, "I should not make a mistake." This will lead to constant disappointment, anger, and feelings of failure and inadequacy. A further issue with should-type thoughts is that we do not always have the control or ability to create what we feel is the right way of being, thus leading to suffering when we or the world continue to be how we are/it is, despite our disagreement. A final issue with "shoulds" is that there are no universal rules as to how we, others, or the world should or should not be. There are no standards we are brought into the world believing that need to be fulfilled, and the standards we do have are those taught to us by people in our environment. These taught "shoulds" also have the ability to take us away from what is true to us, in favor of what we feel we *should* be doing, which can lead to further suffering and detachment from our true self.

If should-type thoughts are helping you to fix something or improve something, continue to use them. If those thoughts are not changing anything, remember the "should" does not really exist; it is an expectation you learned. Let it go and recognize it is a preference but is not an actual life-rule.

Thoughts similar to "should": *should not, must, must not, have to, need, ought to, got to, supposed to*

Common primary emotions before "should": *sad, hurt, dissatisfied, guilty, disappointed, lonely, powerless*

Common resistance emotions stemming from "should": *pressure, anxiety, anger, frustration, hate, resentment, shame*

The Self-Compassion Trap: Self-Pity/Victim Thoughts

In our lives we are faced with challenges, some of us more than others. These challenges can tend to make us feel sad and hurt by others or the world. When we are faced with these emotions in situations, many of us can have a tendency to look at ourselves as victims of life and then wallow in our self-pity. It is a behavioral and thought pattern that is often frowned upon, but does it help in any way?

Self-pity can help in a way where we can give ourselves some level of compassion for our difficult circumstances. It can allow us to feel as though we are comforting ourselves for our difficulties and thus soothing some of the pain attached to those difficulties. If self-pity occurs it will almost always follow the emotions of sadness, hurt, disappointment, dissatisfaction, rejection, abandonment, embarrassment, and loneliness.

Problems with self-pity can arise when one chooses to wallow in "self-compassion"—when we use the self-pity-type thoughts such as *Poor me, my life is so tough* as an excuse to stop living, not take responsibility, and stop taking any action to make our lives better despite the difficult circumstances we may be enduring or have endured. This will then keep us further stuck in self-pity and reinforce our pain and suffering.

Victim mode is similar to self-pity, but in this case, we can have a tendency to look at ourselves as a victim of life or others—as if life is happening to us and victimizing us in some way. We blame the world for the difficulties we have endured or continue to endure and become its victim. This victimhood allows us to relinquish responsibility for creating the life we desire. It may feel like a relief knowing that you are a victim and there is nothing you can do to improve your circumstances and do not have to take responsibility.

The problem here is the time we might spend in victim mode. Not taking responsibility for creating our life, while an initial relief, can mean our life will likely not change and thus we do not create a better version of it. We do not take enough control over the things we can change and choose to get stuck dwelling on those things that have "victimized" us. This will leave us feeling more stuck and thus further victimized and feeling like our life is out of our control, which again leads to more suffering. The other issue with victim mode, particularly when we blame life, is that it is false. Life does not victimize anyone. Life does not have a will of its own to target us with bad things. Living life involves challenges for us all. No one person is more of a victim of it than another because of our challenges.

Common self-pity/victim thoughts:

- *Why me?*
- *It's not fair.*
- *Bad stuff always happens to me.*
- *I can't do anything to make my life better.*
- *Poor me.*
- *My life is really bad.*
- *Why do bad things always happen to me?*
- *Me again!*

Common emotions from victim beliefs:

- Anger
- Resentment
- Hate
- Frustration
- Sadness

Common victim behaviors:

- Giving up
- Getting angry
- Taking revenge

Blame

Most of us like to understand the cause of a situation. The reason is because, by understanding the cause of a situation, we can minimize or enhance the chances of it happening again, depending on whether we like it or dislike it. To understand, though, we must first attribute responsibility to those causes. This is where blame comes into effect. Blame can help us point the finger to the supposed cause of a situation and therefore give us an understanding of it and a direction to go in when looking to the future and its likelihood of repetition. Blame can also be a useful tool to assist us in having a target for our anger in the response to the situation and thus helping us to let the anger go and not keep it stored within our bodies.

Problems with blaming thoughts arise in many ways. One such is the realization that to find the root cause of an event we must return to the beginning of time, which is obviously impossible. In a sense, if we keep blaming something, then we can keep blaming what caused that something and blame the thing prior to the other something. For example, if I blame my mother for me being socially awkward, I then must blame her mother for how my mother is, and then my grandmother's mother for how she was, until my blame reaches all the way back to my first ancestors. This will not work. Blame has no true beginning.

Another issue with blame can occur when there is no one to take responsibility for what has occurred. For example, blaming the government for the policies they have ("Who in the government is responsible?") or wanting to find someone responsible for natural disasters (many people will blame God), or perhaps even blaming an object for my pain ("It's the bed's fault I hurt my foot"). Holding on to blame when there is no one to take responsibility can be harmful and perpetuate anger within us.

The other issue with blame is this: even if we think we have found out who is responsible for the situation and why, we keep holding on to the blame of the person (including ourselves) and use it as an excuse to not move forward in our lives. At the end of the day, we are responsible for living our lives whether someone or something has impacted upon us or not; using blame as a reason to not move on will only be detrimental to us.

If blame helps you understand something so as to not repeat it, then great! Use it, then work on letting the blame go and move on with your life. If it assists in releasing some anger, even if it is for irrational reasons, then that's fine too—take the blame with a grain of salt and see it as a way of releasing anger you feel. But once again, your job is to let it go; otherwise it will consume you and your life.

Blame thoughts:

- *It's their fault.*
- *They should have known better.*
- *How dare they do this to me?*
- *I'm not the cause of the problem—it was...*

The Alternate Reality: If Only/I Wish

If only/I wish-type thoughts generally occur when we are sad or unhappy with the way a situation has turned out. Our mind creates a fantasy about what we would prefer in an attempt to alleviate our shadow emotion. When we are lost in the fantasy, our body reacts to it as if it were true and thus makes us feel better for the moment. In other words, our mind creates an alternate reality to improve our emotional state. For example, if I think: *I wish I had never hurt my back*, I will feel better in the midst of the thought, but then feel worse when I recall the reality of my injured back. *If only* and *I wish* thoughts can also help us to get in touch with what we would like to do differently if we were faced with the same or a similar situation again to get the desired outcome. For example, *If only I had left earlier, I would not be in this traffic* really means: *Next time, I want to leave earlier to avoid the traffic.*

The problem with this type of thinking is that when we return to the reality of what is happening or has happened, we feel worse than we did originally. Our short reprieve from shadow emotions is usually followed by a larger drop back into those same feelings. I wish/If only-type thoughts can also be a problem when we cannot change things for the next time—when no matter how much you wish it could be different, it is not going to change. For example, *I wish my dad had said he loved me before he died.*

If these if only/I wish thoughts are helping you fix something, that's great—keep using them. If not and they are creating more suffering, then stick to the current reality. Ask yourself: how do I feel about the reality of this situation? Then work on being at peace with the emotion and choosing lighter thoughts about it.

Stopping, Leaving, or Quitting Thoughts

Our mind is a natural problem solver, so it offers us solution after solution to our emotional pain. When these solutions do not work, our mind will then give us the options of stopping, leaving, or quitting the thing causing the emotional pain. Stopping, leaving, or quitting thoughts will likely occur for most people after prolonged feelings of emotional pain with no obvious solution to improve them, but can also occur at first sight of pain within us. The thought of stopping, leaving, or quitting whatever is causing the emotional pain makes us feel a sense of relief that the pain will soon be over. For example, feeling the relief of knowing you will be leaving a job you hate. Suicidal thoughts can be deemed as quitting/leaving thoughts. They occur within our mind as supposed solutions to the pain we are enduring. That is: *If I was not around, I would not be feeling so bad.* Thoughts of leaving, stopping, or quitting can be useful thoughts in that they can let us know the right time to stop trying to make things better and leave or accept a situation. They can assist in knowing when the right time to quit is, especially if we do not have control over changing the situation. They can help us minimize our emotional pain by motivating us to withdraw from the situation creating it. Our mind tends to assume *If I stopped doing this, then I would not feel the emotional pain.*

Problems with these types of thoughts can occur when our low tolerance for any emotional pain makes us stop, leave, or quit too soon when a level of perseverance would assist in changing the situation. That is, we end up quitting when the going gets tough and do not then achieve the things we set out to achieve. Problems also occur when they become suicidal thoughts, our mind's way of trying to solve the pain we are in. Everything is transient and forever changing; acting on these types of thoughts can prevent us from working through our emotional pain and making it through to the other side of it. There is also a huge conclusion we jump to when we have these thoughts, namely that our pain stops when we die. But we do not know if this is true.

If leaving thoughts are helping you make a decision that feels true to you to get out of a difficult situation, then it may be a good idea to utilize their advice and move toward a better situation. If they are trying to motivate you to leave a situation at a bad time, or it does not align with your inner truth, then thank your mind for trying to help, but you're choosing to stick this one out, change your perceptions and work through the emotions that come with it.

Common stopping, quitting, leaving thoughts:

- *I can't do it anymore.*
- *I'm sick of this.*
- *It's just too hard.*
- *I'm over it all.*
- *I just want to go away.*
- *I want to die.*
- *I wish I was dead.*
- *It would be easier if I was not here.*

Judgment of Emotions

Perceptions of right/wrong, good/bad, better/worse, strong/weak are different types of judgments we hold within our minds. They can also form the basis of the core beliefs we have about our emotions. Many of us have learned that it is right or wrong to feel a certain emotion, or good or bad to do a certain behavior, and depending on what we have learned we can judge ourselves accordingly when we feel the emotion or engage in emotional behaviors. But where did these beliefs come from? None of us were born with any beliefs or judgments about our emotions or actions. They are repeated thoughts we have absorbed due to our interactions within our environment, emotions, and bodily reactions. Much like a sponge will absorb some of the water if it is submerged; we will absorb what it is we are taught from others. These beliefs are deep-seated patterns of thinking that color the way we look at our emotional world. If we were to look at emotions without the filter of our beliefs, we would see the exact same things. Instead, we interpret these emotions through our beliefs and react accordingly. Interpreting our emotions and behaviors through our judgments can tend to help us or hinder us.

At birth, we are born with our instincts and temperament, as well as our innate personality and emotional reactivity. What we are not born with are beliefs. If a child feels hungry, they will cry until their needs are met. They would not believe that they would die if they did not eat, as they have not learned the concept of death. If they had learned the concept of death, they still might not fear it unless the child was taught that death was a "bad" thing.

Through the interactions with our parents or caregivers we will begin learning the belief patterns from those people in relation to our emotions and behaviors. These beliefs will then trigger differing emotional reactions within us when we are already feeling an emotion. Because we've learned that feeling a certain way is wrong or bad, we feel guilty or perhaps ashamed about how we feel. How often has another person told you "You shouldn't be feeling like that" or "Emotion is a sign of weakness"? If this was a common thing you have heard, there is a high probability you will judge yourself poorly every time you feel an emotion and you will attempt to negate it, even though it is a valid feeling.

If we felt a pleasant emotion, we may have learned it is a good thing; an unpleasant emotion means it is a bad thing. Thus, beliefs of good and bad in relation to emotions form in us. As a result of these beliefs, as we conform to what we have been taught is good or bad, our behavior changes and our ability to behave as our true self dissipates. Throughout the first seven years of life most of the foundational core beliefs about ourselves, our emotions, and the world are established. While we can still change and adopt new beliefs throughout our lives, they tend to emerge more slowly.

But where do beliefs about emotions originate from if we are not born with them? Because if we were not born with them, then our parents must not have been born with theirs, and so on and so on. Beliefs are formed within us, the outcome of lessons learned from parents, caregivers, siblings, school, friends, media, society, religion, and culture. As we do not know any better as children if we are taught otherwise, we can have a tendency to adopt these beliefs from the outside world. This will then, in turn, create an emotional reaction within us. For example, if I'm taught it is weak to cry, then if I do cry, I feel ashamed about it (very common in males). If repeated, these beliefs become further reinforced and more deeply seated as true. This is how beliefs begin in every person.

If beliefs have no truly identifiable origin and we did not choose the ones we have, can we know which ones serve us?

The first thing to realize here is *there are no true beliefs*. There is no such thing as right or wrong, good or bad, better or worse. They are a bunch of thoughts in our mind passed down from generation to generation as a way to "assist" us in making sense of our emotional states. Beliefs about our environment, ourselves, and others are not ultimately true. They are merely thoughts which pop up in our minds and the truth exists without having to label it with a thought. We normally feel that the thought itself is the truth, though, because we have been taught to give words absolute truth and also because our emotional body agrees with it. When we have no thoughts in our minds, the reality exists as it is. It is only when we have a thought that we confuse the thought with the reality, and emotions habitually follow, reinforcing our belief in the thought.

If there are no true thoughts, is everything pointless? If you have come to this conclusion, you do not understand how to utilize your belief patterns as tools to assist you, instead of all the governing ideas of the world and its functioning. Learning about good and bad, right and wrong, is deeply personal to each individual. But seeing the world more clearly and aligning our belief patterns to those facts helps us respond with more alignment when emotions arise. Our job is to realize there is no such thing as a good or bad emotion; they are normal functions. There is no need to feel ashamed, guilty or disappointed for feeling a certain way, and emotion is not an indication of weakness.

Recognizing there are no absolute true beliefs will set us free to be ourselves and connect with our emotions. If you find yourself judging yourself for your emotional states, it might be helpful to think twice and truly decide what you want to believe about emotions, not necessarily what you have been taught. In general, if the belief provides a sense of peace, it is in alignment with the ultimate truth.

Critical Thoughts (Self-Criticism/Criticism of Others)

Our mind's job is not only to analyze situations but also to analyze ourselves to ensure we are not subjecting ourselves to emotional pain. So, critical-type thoughts serve the purpose of berating us in an attempt to learn and push away those parts of ourselves which are causing our pain. This is also the same for criticism of others. If we criticize someone, then we are attempting to control them through disapproval and rejection in order to encourage them to push their "problematic" behavior or quality away. Critical thoughts tend to create emotions of anger, hate, frustration, and resentment which can have the power to change or repel.

The benefit of critical thoughts or critique is that they can make us aware of where growth and change could be beneficial. Without the ability to self-reflect with critique, we would only be able to look at ourselves in a positive light and thus we would never grow, change, or repel any behaviors which do not serve us in living as our true selves. The same also applies for criticism or critique of others, done in a loving way to help them grow.

Problems occur with critical thinking when they go beyond critique which is helping us to move forward, and lead to tearing down or shaming ourselves or another into growing or punishment. Critical thoughts can have the ability to demotivate us and tear away at our sense of self-esteem and worth. They can also generate self-hate and hate of others, which then pushes us further away from ourselves. Critical-type thoughts can also be problematic in that we may have learned that a certain behavior/quality/trait is bad/wrong/undesirable and this makes us change something about ourselves which does not need to be changed. In turn, we would get further away from our true selves and be led into a level of conditional self-love or acceptance—where we can only accept ourselves if we do no "wrong" (which as I've already mentioned does not exist, and even if it did, with us being fallible humans it would be impossible to achieve).

Critical thinking will generally come secondary to the emotions of guilt, disappointment, rejection, abandonment, low self-worth, and hurt as a means to try to solve them. These emotions are designed to make us self-reflect. The types of self-reflection and criticism will be dependent on how we have learned to cope with these emotions, predominantly as a child. If we were taught self-compassion, our level of self-criticism will likely be low. If we were taught through criticism and high expectations, our criticism of self and others will normally be high. Because it has been going on for a long time, self-criticism is familiar, even if it does not serve us. There is usually a part of us that thinks we need to continue to hate ourselves so as to learn and move forward with our lives. If we do not decide to change the way we want to relate to ourselves, criticism will continue to be the tool used to attempt to change and thus continue to create problems for us.

If some level of criticism or critique is helping you to love your life and grow and is done in a self-compassionate and encouraging way, then continue to use it. If criticism is hindering you and causing you to have a bad, hateful relationship with yourself or others, then it may be useful to drop the criticism and start learning, accepting, forgiving, encouraging, and teaching yourself or others in a kind, compassionate way.

Common critical thoughts:

- *I'm an idiot.*
- *That was so dumb.*
- *Why would I/you do that?*
- *I am/You are/That is so stupid.*
- *I'm a bad person.*

Common emotions from critical thoughts:

- Anger
- Resentment
- Shame
- Hate
- Frustration

Common critical behaviors:

- Giving up
- Getting angry
- Shaming or judging self or others
- Overdoing things
- Self-denial
- Self-harm

Questioning: Who? What? When? Where? Why? How?

At some point in our lives, we all question things. In fact, at school we are taught to always ask who, what, when, where, why, and how when it comes to gathering information and basic problem solving. The answers to these questions can help us to get a more complete picture of an event or situation and allow us to feel secure in the knowledge of having a clearer understanding.

As humans we have an innate desire to understand and make sense of things that happen. We dislike uncertainty and confusion and instead feel more secure in ourselves and our lives when we know the answers to the things that trouble us. Understanding the answers can leave us feeling safe, secure, and calmer overall. Evolutionarily speaking, knowing the answers meant that we would be less inclined to encounter a dangerous situation when we understood what caused it, when it was likely to occur, who caused it, where it would take place, why it happened, and how it happened in the first place. It is for this reason we developed the ability to question situations and events, to assist us in learning from the current situation and to avoid making the same mistakes again. Asking these questions can be helpful for us if we can find the answers. In our life, knowing these answers can help us make sense of the beliefs and emotions we have by giving us a reason for their presence, and possibly even changing them and removing whatever is triggering these emotions within us.

Unfortunately, we do not always know the answers to these questions. We have heard the saying, "Life works in mysterious ways." This really means we do not know the answers for who, what, when, where, why, and how. Asking questions for which an answer, especially a definitive answer, does not exist only serves to create further emotional suffering. Not only will it reinforce the uncertainty and helplessness we already feel, but it will most likely lead to feelings of anxiety, anger, and frustration as we attempt to control what we cannot control.

If you are able to ask these questions and get an answer, then keep using these tools you have learned. They can be good ways to assist us in feeling better and making sense of the world around us. If you are asking these questions in response to a situation where these answers do not exist, then it is important to stop asking and be okay with feelings of uncertainty or confusion. It may also be helpful for you to work on accepting helplessness and recognizing you cannot always have all the answers.

Common emotions before this questioning:

- Uncertainty
- Vulnerability
- Helplessness
- Confusion
- Hurt
- Disappointment
- Rejection

Common behaviors:

- Searching/researching
- Constantly asking questions to yourself or others

Logical/Rational Thinking

Logical thinking is what many of us have learned. It's what we have been taught to do at school, in our society, and in our lives. It is where most people in society point to when the goal is having a "realistic" mental outlook. It is the process of using facts, evidence, or reasoning to come to a conclusion about a situation in order to help with understanding it. Just think logically or rationally and everything will be explained—everything will feel better. When it comes to a particular situation, if we think logically or rationally enough about it then the situation will not affect us, and we will be able to move on with our lives untroubled.

Logical thinking can be effective at helping us to understand and not make a situation bigger than it is (catastrophize). Being rational about a situation can help with making sense of it by putting things about the situation into some form of order. The structure that is created by rational/logical thinking can lead us to a sense of calm due to everything fitting into that sense of order. Logical/rational thinking shapes our belief patterns about the world. Order represents a sense of safety to us as we know what to expect and have the ability to explain it. When we have the ability to explain it in such an orderly way, it then helps us to decide how to predict it and therefore prepare for the next time. Having a sense of logical/rational thinking about things can give us a greater understanding of how the world works so that our expectations are more shaped by reality rather than by opinion.

Problems with rational/logical thinking occur for numerous reasons. One such reason is that situations in the world do not always make logical sense to us. If the situation falls outside of the realm of our logic, it will tend to make us more confused and possibly even angry as the situation does not agree with our belief system; an example is a person saying, "I shouldn't be feeling this way," when clearly they are already "feeling this way." The other problem with logical thinking is it does not account for how we feel about a situation.

Our emotions do not always respond to logic/rational thinking. Trying to use logic to talk ourselves out of an emotion can suppress the emotion and behaviors that come with it or cause us to feel guilty or disappointed in our inability to control the emotion. An example of this is if you felt sad because someone you loved had died, you might tell yourself "It's good that they are not suffering" as a way to feel less sad. This can suppress the sadness and stop you from grieving, thus creating more grief long term, or it can make you feel guilty for not feeling better at that thought. Rational thinking can also take away and strip us of our ability to feel emotions. Stereotypically, men are more logical than women and have trouble understanding their own emotional states because they are not "logical." Rational thinking strips reality down to mere thoughts and does not allow the wonder and essence of reality to penetrate into us emotionally.

Imagine and feel the wonder of seeing the birth of a child through emotion. Now imagine it through logic: "There are children born all the time. It is just a natural process. Another child born in the world." Notice how numbness occurs. The same can be said for anything you are passionate about. Watching a sporting game through logic/rational thinking means we feel no emotion and thus do not invest in what it is we are partaking in. Instead we are creating an "It is what it is" attitude about situations and life. While a truer statement has never been stated, "It is what it is" does not question further to the point of asking, "How does 'what it is' make me feel?"

The other problem with logic is there is no true definition of what is logical or not logical. It will change from person to person, society to society, and culture to culture. Thus, one logical thought might be true to one person, but not true to another.

Logical thinking can be helpful in terms of making sense of reality and interpreting it to gain a sense of calm and security, while minimizing an emotional reaction. It can help address the world for what it is and can thus help us react accordingly if required. If overused, it suppresses our emotions, takes away our passion, and creates a dullness in us which can reduce our inner light. So, logical/rational thinking is best done when combined with emotional awareness. When we are able to connect with our emotion within the situation and allow it to be, we can also connect with logical/rational thinking if required to make sense of the situation and to change our actions to reflect our truest desires.

Common logical-type thoughts:

- *It is what it is.*
- *It is not worth worrying about the past.*
- *Don't worry about things you can't change.*
- *It's better off this way.*
- *It's not true.*
- *Shit happens.*
- *It's not that bad.*
- Fact stating in response to an emotion.

Positive Thinking

"Just think positive and you will be okay" is a suggestion most of us have heard many times in our lives. I know I have. We're told that if we focus on being positive, we are guaranteed to feel better. If you have positive thoughts or can just be a positive person you will be happy, and no problems will affect you at all. On top of that, be sure to avoid negativity or having negative thoughts because they are by their very nature negative or bad and will definitely lead to unhappiness. This is the attitude society often has toward our positive and negative thoughts. Thinking negative is bad and thinking positive is good.

Positive thinking definitely has a place in helping us to have a more fulfilling and satisfying life. Thinking positive can assist us in having hope and direction for our future. It also creates a sense of motivation within us to help us persevere with whatever is important to us. Positive thinking can also assist us in seeing the brighter side of a situation (or the proverbial silver lining)—giving us a more balanced view of the situation at hand. It can also help us reframe how we look at the world and focus on the pleasant things which occur or exist instead of the unpleasant things. Positive thinking can also assist us in manifesting our wants and desires to create the lives we truly yearn for, as long as it is utilized with trust and faith. So, as far as positive thinking goes, it can be a great benefit to our lives when used in the correct manner.

However, problems with positive thinking can easily arise. One major problem with it is when it is used to cover up an emotion and pretend we do not feel the way we feel. For example: *It's for the best* might be used to cover up a person's disappointment at missing a job opportunity. If we definitely felt it was for the best, we would not have felt the disappointment in the first place, but rather a sense of relief. Another issue with positive thinking is when it is used to predict the future and let us know *everything is going to be alright, everything will work out just fine*. If we truly believed these thoughts, then our uncertainty would be eliminated, and we would never have any fear of the future. Positive thinking in this situation would feel like lying to yourself because there is a deeper part of you that knows you cannot predict the future and definitely do not know everything will be "fine." Positive thinking can also be superimposed onto an underlying negative belief pattern. For example, *"I am good just as I am"* is used to overwrite *"I am not good enough."* Our emotions respond to the most deep-seated belief, so superimposing a positive thought over the old one does not replace it because we do not believe it. It is important to both utilize and understand what type of "negative" belief or thought you are having and why you are having it before you can replace it with a lighter one you can believe. Positive thinking can also be a way to deny or bypass the release of an emotion. Allowing ourselves to think "negative" can assist us in processing how we feel and to grieve the emotion that has been triggered in us. In fact, allowing ourselves to have some "negative" thoughts as we release an emotion can be cathartic and healing.

If positive thinking is assisting you in moving forward with your life, if it is helping you manifest your desires or see the balanced side of a situation, utilize it. If it is blocking your emotions, facilitating lying to yourself or trying to eliminate a belief system, then it may be best to sit with the emotion rather than trying to control it. Overall, it is better to grow lighter, believable perceptions in a situation than to force yourself to think positive thoughts. We can feel the emotion and still lighten how we approach life.

Types of positive thoughts:

- *Everything will be fine.*
- *It will work out alright.*
- *It's for the best.*
- *Just look on the bright side.*
- *It will be okay.*
- *Everything is perfect just as it is.*
- Stating a belief that is opposite from the one you have.

Affirmations

Affirmations are similar to positive or logical thoughts. They differ only in that they are repeated in an attempt to change how we think and consequently feel about a situation.

Affirmations can be useful in creating these changes, particularly if we can understand the origins of the beliefs and can truly see the falseness of the beliefs we are trying to change. It is also important to use affirmations we find believable and not ones we feel are false. If we try to use an affirmation we do not believe, then we will resist it, and therefore not take it on board.

Overall, affirmations used as an attempt to control emotions are not long-term solutions for the emotions. It is best to sit with the emotion and arrive at the truth through the emotion, rather than try to force the emotion away. For example, trying to replace my initial belief and feeling of not being good enough with the affirmation "I am good enough just as I am" will inevitably create a suppression of the not-good-enough feeling and not solve it. If I am aware of the beliefs that cause me to feel not good enough, and am okay to sit with the emotion of not good enough, then an affirmation can be useful to create the new reality and new belief system, minimizing the longer-term arising of the emotion for the situation.

So, use affirmations if they work for you. If you are only using them to try to control an emotion, make peace with it first, then work toward changing the beliefs through lighter affirmations that are believable to you.

Comparing

We are living in a world where there is no actual definition of success. Because no definition exists, success then is a relative concept. In essence we can only define our success/failure when we judge it compared to another person or group. Comparing is a natural way to function; it allows us to engage society's and our expectations of "success."

Comparisons can be useful at times to assist us in determining what others have and looking at ourselves and what we may require to attain the same things. Comparisons can also help motivate us to strive toward a goal and to "succeed" at whatever we feel is important to us. Comparisons can also help us decide what we do not want when we see it in others.

Problems with comparisons arise for numerous reasons. Comparing ourselves with others is not fair on ourselves. We were born to different parents, have different DNA, different personalities, have had different life-experiences, different opportunities, and overall, vastly different lives. When comparing ourselves to another person it is impossible for our minds to calculate all that went into them having what they have. In a true comparison, all things must be equal, and obviously with our lives they are not. It is also incredibly unfair and inaccurate to assume we are less than someone else because we do not have what they have, or more than someone else because we have something the other does not. The other issue with comparisons is that they are trying to attain an ideal level of success which does not exist; they are standards based on conditioned lessons and will differ from person to person.

Comparisons work well when they are achievable, helping us to see what we want based on what another person has, and reflecting upon how we may be getting it in our own way. They also work well to look at avoiding having or doing what another has or does, so as to grow and improve a certain behavior. Comparisons do not work when we cannot get what the other has due to our vastly different lives, and also do not work when the standard of "success" we are chasing does not exist.

Emotions before comparisons:

- Sadness
- Disappointment
- Low self-worth
- Rejection
- Abandonment
- Dissatisfaction

Resistance emotions after comparisons:

- Jealousy
- Envy
- Hate
- Self-hate
- Lower self-worth
- Frustration
- Anger
- Resentment

Comparison thoughts:

- *They have more than me.*
- *They make more money than me.*
- *I am better than them.*
- *At least I have a pretty face.*
- *If only I had their body.*
- *I'm less than them.*

***

As you can see, there are many types of emotional control thinking patterns which our conditioned egoic mind has learned through the experiences in our lives. These thinking patterns can assist our true self in loving ourselves by trying to control our emotional states. They can sometimes make us feel more pleasant and avoid feeling unpleasant and at times be useful to us. It is important to be aware of our thoughts and vigilant in seeing if they are helping us live our truest life or if they are creating more pain and suffering. Conditioned egoic thoughts are our internal behaviors for controlling emotions, but we also have external behaviors for controlling them in order to feel better or more familiar.

Chapter Eleven

Conditioned Egoic Behaviors

I enjoy watching television and movies. I could spend a whole day lying on my sofa barely moving and zoning out whatever is going on in the world and, more importantly, whatever is going on in my mind and body. In other words, television is a really good distraction for me when I have problems I'm not ready or able to deal with. But what if I always lay around watching TV any time I had a problem? What if that was my only coping strategy? I'm sure my life would go downhill really fast.

While egoic thoughts are internal control strategies, conditioned egoic behaviors are physical actions we take to minimize and control our emotions. There are infinite types of these actions. Many of them are connected to certain emotions and they usually work in conjunction with the egoic thoughts. These behaviors are often driven by emotional states and can assist us in feeling better when they work well. Yet they tend to create more true-self disconnection and suffering for us longer term when they do not work well or are used habitually and unconsciously. The problem with conditioned egoic behaviors revolves around what they cost in terms of how we live our lives. While these costs vary from person to person, they often include missed experiences, time, energy, health, freedom, relationships, vitality, money, more emotional pain, and more. Most important, they are not always in alignment with the calling of the true self. As we know, there are infinite types of these behaviors, so I will mention but a few of the common ones we use to attempt to feel "better."

Avoidance

Avoidance is the action of keeping away from or not doing something. It is a type of behavior we use to escape from situations, people, or even thoughts that cause us to feel the shadow emotions. It is a common tool useful to prevent emotional or physical pain for us in situations we assume will create it. It is a behavior often motivated by the anxiety family of emotions.

Avoidance as a behavior can protect us and prevent us from encountering situations which may be harmful or dangerous. Avoiding a place where we have previously been attacked can enhance our chances of survival and minimize our overall threat levels. Avoidance can also assist in minimizing our likelihood of overwhelming ourselves in situations which have the propensity to do so. Think about how avoiding or postponing some household chores or work tasks can temporarily reduce stress. Avoidance can also be helpful if you need a way out of situations you do not wish to encounter—like walking across the street when you see a troublesome neighbor or aggressive dog. Avoidance can be a useful ally in helping us keep safe and feeling pleasant. Mostly, though, avoidance can assist in preventing us from encountering situations that make us feel the shadow emotions.

Problems with avoidance can definitely arise and are well documented. The main issue with avoidance is it is often overused, which limits our ability to live a rich, full life of our truest self. Avoiding situations that make us scared and feeling unpleasant can come at a huge cost to our lives. Avoiding shopping centers or driving can stop us living a meaningful life; avoiding communication or confrontations with people can create long-term friction, more hurt, and especially resentment. Avoidance of important and meaningful situations, while initially decreasing stress, also results in an increase in our stress/pressure level in the longer term. Avoidance of disappointment can mean we do not try anything and thus end up feeling more disappointment, and it stops us getting what we want. Avoidance of guilt can sometimes mean we live life to such high standards we burn ourselves out. Also, avoidance of emotions means we store them in our body for longer periods of time.

If avoidance is helping to keep you safe from a situation you do not wish to face, or from an emotion you do not wish to feel, then great—continue to avoid. If it is keeping you away from doing what is true to you and leaving you unfulfilled, then it may be worth taking a chance, facing the situation and doing something more meaningful.

Common types of avoidance behaviors include people-pleasing, perfectionism, procrastination, quitting, opting out, not trying, escaping and withdrawing, and passivity.

Anxiety is the emotion that usually motivates avoidance, and at its deepest level avoidance is often motivated by a desire to circumvent feeling any of the primary emotions we may be sensitive to in a specific situation.

Common internal-control thinking patterns which precede avoidance are: worry, "shoulds" (for self) and stopping/leaving/quitting thoughts. Therefore, if you are engaging in problematic avoidance, it would be useful to learn how to make peace with the emotions you are trying to avoid and face things one step at a time.

Aggression

Not only do we all experience anger at times, but we all have moments when we become aggressive, whether it be toward others or ourselves. Aggression is a part of our genetic makeup. It is the fight behavior in the "fight, flight, or freeze" response within us all—the system within us that is designed to use force to help us to protect ourselves or to get our needs met. It helps us feel better and stronger and in a position of power instead of feeling weak and powerless.

Aggression can help us to protect ourselves and keep others from taking advantage of us. It can help with standing strong to get our needs met and with exerting our will to ensure we are able to give to ourselves without unreasonable sacrifice.

Aggression's uses can be over utilized, which creates problems within relationships and within ourselves. Many people who overuse aggression tend to have volatile lives and volatile relationships. They tend to use aggression to cover up their more vulnerable feelings and thus attempt to dominate the other person, leading either to arguments or to feelings of fear from the more submissive person. The excessively aggressive person is usually a poor compromiser who wants everything their way. Someone may also make themselves the target of their own aggression in an attempt to self-motivate. When we turn our aggression on ourselves, we treat ourselves in a hostile, domineering way and use hate and criticism to motivate ourselves. Any overuse of aggression is definitely not living in alignment with the true self and will eventually lead to issues and come at a cost to our lives and most likely those around us.

Another problem with aggression is that the power is short-lived and does not make us feel better long term. To keep getting the power hit, we need to continue to be aggressive and exert our perceived control over ourselves, another person, or the situation. This is unhealthy for us and keeps us stuck in a state of aggression.

Aggression-type behaviors: intimidation, being condescending, hostility, revenge seeking, smashing things, screaming, swearing, fighting, violence, arguing, being argumentative, being defensive, confronting others, manipulating, name calling, murder, harming others, meanness, passive aggression, rudeness.

Aggression will almost exclusively come out when a person is feeling one of the angry emotions. If you commonly experience aggression, it will be beneficial for you to know how to make peace with and allow the primary emotions that aggression is attempting to cover up—especially powerlessness, sadness, disappointment, and hurt.

Distraction

"Just keep yourself busy" is a common piece of advice I often hear. "Just focus on doing your work, or go out for a walk—it will do you wonders." Distraction too is a behavior we use to try to feel good and to avoid having unpleasant feelings and egoic thoughts.

When we put our attention onto something other than what is bothering us, it can offer us a reprieve from our emotional pain as well as from the constant barrage of emotional thinking we are using in attempts to solve our emotions. In this way, distraction can be a useful tool to assist in coping with our emotions and thoughts. When we keep busy and keep our mind focused on an activity, our thoughts and emotions cease to exist for a period of time.

While it can prove helpful, it can also be detrimental to our overall wellbeing. Continuously distracting ourselves to feel better can be tiring and unremitting. We must keep going to keep chasing away the feelings and thoughts. This can tire us out, exhaust us, and lead to burnout. The other issue with distraction is that it doesn't remove the emotion—it suppresses it; and the moment we stop distracting ourselves the emotion and thoughts return, usually with a vengeance.

Common types of distraction behaviors: overworking, watching TV, eating, doing exercise, chores, partying, shopping, reading, gaming, internet, social media, socializing, cell phones, drinking alcohol, and many others.

Distraction is a common behavior that can occur following any of the emotions outlined in this book. If you find you are distracting yourself, ask: *What emotion am I trying to distract myself from?* Then practice making peace with that emotion.

Chasing the Light/Chasing Away the Shadow

Another way in which we attempt to control our emotions is by chasing the light. Chasing the light is using something to quickly shift from a shadow emotion to a light emotion. When I feel sad or down I will sometimes treat myself to a chocolate or coffee or indulge in a dessert, which makes me feel better, at least for a moment. We tend to chase the light in two ways. One way is when we are already feeling the shadow emotion and wish to feel the light. The other way is when we feel neutral and wish we could feel a lighter emotion. We use many things to chase away our shadow feelings. These can include (but are not limited to) food, caffeine, exercise, gambling, drugs, alcohol, nicotine, medication, antidepressants, vitamins, supplements, herbal remedies, people, sex, shopping, achieving, working hard, striving, exerting, seeking approval, purposefully triggering others, and meditation. These things—some of which are more beneficial than others at times—all have the ability to assist us in feeling better and thus we can have a tendency to continue to use them. If used in moderation and without creating harm, these things can be helpful from the perspective of offering short-term relief.

If overused, these things can become addictions and create further problems in our lives. The problem with chasing the light is that it does not work as a long-term solution to dealing with our emotions—because we do not have full control over them, so we, in turn, end up losing control of ourselves and our behaviors in trying to control our emotions. We end up becoming a slave to the behavior. Chasing the light also becomes problematic because to sustain the feeling, we must keep chasing forever and need ever more to sustain our "light" emotion. The desire becomes insatiable, and thus we continue on the never-ending cycle at a huge cost to our life and disconnection from our truth. Another issue with chasing the hit is the possible health detriment caused by such behaviors, such as excessive weight gain from overeating, lung cancer from smoking, loss of health from drug or alcohol use, loss of money and lifestyle from gambling.

If you find yourself partaking in a light/shadow-chasing behavior, it is useful to ask: *What emotion am I trying to get rid of? What emotion am I trying to attain?* Then again practice making peace with the emotions you have now.

Self-Sabotage/Self-Preservation

Self-sabotage is when we consciously or unconsciously engage in behaviors which prevent us from achieving what it is we want to achieve. Deep down we all want to feel pleasant emotions, but many of us can be scared to experience the emotions we want. It doesn't make sense, does it? At least not until we look more deeply. If we are chasing something that would make us feel proud or successful, we must be ready for possible feelings of disappointment or feeling like a failure. The idea of becoming successful and then possibly losing that success becomes so overwhelmingly scary that we engage in self-sabotage to return to a familiar emotional state which does not involve the risk of failing. We can do this for many emotions and become so uneasy at the thought of losing the emotion we truly want to feel that we do something contradictory to our goals in order to return to a sense of security and familiarity, no matter how limiting it is to our life. Self-sabotage is a warped form of self-protection or preservation we engage in to minimize possible emotional pain.

Self-sabotage behaviors can be numerous and plentiful. They can range from picking an argument all the way to self-harm behaviors. Overall, the purpose of self-sabotage behaviors is to attempt to bring about a more familiar emotion, as the anticipation of feeling worse or getting what we want creates too much anxiety for us to manage in the moment. If you notice you are self-sabotaging, it may be helpful to see what emotions frighten you, and practice allowing them to exist in your body.

***

With conditioned egoic thoughts and behaviors that we have been doing for a long time, it will normally take time for us to do them less or stop doing them. This is because they have a momentum within us that continues even when we are aware of some of the problems they cause. Be kind to yourself as you notice yourself doing things that might seem destructive even though you know better. *Knowing* better does not always mean being able to *do* better. The momentum of your habitual actions will slow in time, and it will become easier to enact your new knowledge.

***

To embody the full wisdom of when to use the egoic thoughts or behavior strategies to best live our life as a true self, we must first know the emotions we have. We must understand why we have them, the role they play in our lives, our responses to them, and also the ways they can serve us to live as our true selves. In doing so, we will also learn about the problems that can occur when we identify with them or do not know how to utilize them for our truest life.

SECTION 4

The Emotions

In the following chapters I discuss the emotions—innate uses and purposes. Each emotion has a distinct function and set of behaviors they motivate us toward that may assist in our functioning as our true self. Depending upon our conditioned egoic mind, our responses to them, and identification with them, they also have the ability to create much suffering for us. Our goal in understanding our emotions is to learn to differentiate between those triggered by our true self in order to help us function and those created by our conditioning which may not assist us in having a life of wellbeing connected to our true self.

I have divided emotions into different groups, or "families" as I like to call them. These are:

Happy/Sad
Pleased/Hurt
Relationship-with-Self
Relaxed/Anxious
Calm/Angry
Freeze-Response

In general, the happy/sad, pleased/hurt, and relationship-with-self family of emotions are our primary sets of emotions. They are our most vulnerable feelings and thus leave us feeling tender and exposed when they occur.

Anxiety, anger, and freeze-response families are more resistant emotions. They are designed to save our lives or to minimize the pain of the primary emotions. When not saving our lives, the anxiety family of emotions is usually secondary—a way to prevent feeling the primary emotions. The anger family usually comes secondary as a way to help us get rid of or solve the primary emotions. And the freeze-response family comes secondary as a way to dampen the pain of the primary emotions to a manageable level. Noticing the emotion we feel and when it arises can minimize our suffering and wake us up to our true self in any situation.

While the emotions have been divided into their families, it is important to realize that any emotion we feel is just one end of a continuum of its opposite emotion. Although they appear to be opposite emotions, they are not two distinct emotions but one emotion with two sides, like two sides of one coin. Therefore, happy and sad are a single emotion on an emotional continuum, just like feeling pleased or hurt or any of the other emotions I discuss in this book. It is impossible for us to know one side of the emotion without the relative point of the other side. In general, feeling the shadow side of the emotion will motivate us to do something to move toward the light end on the continuum.

So far, you have learned how to connect to your true self, find and change your beliefs to align with your truth, identify conditioned egoic thoughts and behaviors, allow emotions, and practice self-love techniques. In this section I explore how to label emotions, be aware of their uses, actively navigate through them, and put together the knowledge you have gathered in this book with the intention of converting it to wisdom. Wisdom is the ability to apply knowledge, and without application, no amount of knowledge will make a difference in our lives or help us live from our true self. The more we apply the knowledge, the more we create new pathways and responses to improve our connection with our true self and make our lives more peaceful.

At the end of each consideration of an emotion is a step-by-step guide to working through that emotion so you can apply the knowledge and practices to convert it into wisdom.

Chapter Twelve

The Happy/Sad Family of Emotions

Happy/Sad

Everyone is going to feel sad at some point in their lives. It is from sadness that we are triggered to try to seek happiness. Happiness is at the opposite end of the continuum to sadness. It is through knowing what makes us sad that we are able to garner motivation to move toward what it is that makes us happy. While feeling happy is a lot more pleasant for us, to live as our true self it is important to learn how to allow ourselves to feel sad.

Sadness is the emotion I find people either struggle with most, or try their best to avoid. We live in a society where we are constantly told to cheer up, be positive, or be happy—where we are taught to think about what makes us happy and do our best to get it. Everything taught to us from a young age is designed to motivate us to chase happiness. Most people, when asked what they want for their lives, answer with a simple "I want to be happy." While this can be a useful mentality, we often adopt it at the expense of learning and knowing how to allow sadness to exist. After all, there will be times in our lives where nothing we do will work to solve the sad emotion when it arises. Just think of losing a loved one through death, or perhaps finding out that your child has a rare illness that affects their quality of life (or imagine the same for yourself). Avoiding sadness in these instances (and many others) may be impossible, so our taught lessons of chasing away sadness end up creating more suffering. That is, unless we learn how to respect sadness and use it in the way it was designed to be used.

Imagine for a moment a life without sadness. Only knowing the feeling of happiness. Seems ideal at first thought, doesn't it? Without sadness, however, we would not know what happiness was. We would not have a relative point of emotion to compare our happiness to. It is impossible to know happiness without sadness. They are opposite ends of the same emotion. Plus, knowing what makes us sad/happy is also useful to guide us toward what feels good and away from what feels bad. It is like an emotional compass guiding us toward the life most true to us and what we sincerely want.

Apart from motivating us to chase happiness, sadness is the emotion that can assist us in releasing any emotional pain we may be suffering. If we were to think of a sad memory from the past, allowing ourselves to feel sad would assist us in coming to a place of acceptance as the pain releases. Or perhaps you may feel sad about a recent loss, or the state of affairs in the world today (illness, war, famine, political leaders). Allowing the sad feeling to arise within you, without perpetuating it (through conditioned egoic thoughts or behaviors), is your body and mind's way of releasing the pain attached to the event or situation you feel sad about.

Everyone experiences emotions differently. Generally, sadness depresses our bodily functions. Physically we may feel heavier, our movements get slower, we lose motivation, we lose energy, our zest for life is lower, we have heaviness or pain in our chest, feeling like we want to cry, have pressure behind our eyes, and many other symptoms and sensations which are personal to each of us. These symptoms and sensations of sadness are designed to motivate the mind and body to release the pain of sadness. The body slows down to stop and reduce distraction so that the mind is able to reflect upon what is causing the sadness. This reflection allows the feelings of sadness to arise; even more so, the emotion is able to be released from your body. The body and mind are attempting to purge the sadness. The only way to purge it is to "feel it out"—to allow your body to have these unpleasant feelings without overly attempting to reduce their intensity. There are no short cuts in releasing sadness; there are no magic pills to take sadness away. Only allowing the sensations and symptoms of sadness and time will do this.

What makes you feel sad will be personal to you. You may find you get sad about things that no one else gets sad about, or perhaps you share many similar sad situations. The true self will at times utilize sadness to cleanse our body of pain. If this is the case, be okay to let the sadness exist. Other times, it will utilize sadness to help motivate us toward creating what we truly want. In this case we may need to be brave enough to take action or patient enough to take action at the most suitable time and pace. However, being okay with feeling sad gives us the option to choose which action is the truest in the situation.

Here are some other emotions with similar functions to sad:

- unhappy
- heartbroken
- despondent
- devastated
- down
- joyless
- low
- miserable
- upset
- grief-stricken

Here is a list of emotions for happy:

- joyous
- pleased

- encouraged
- good
- excited
- elated
- cheerful
- delighted

Creating an aligned pathway to deal with sadness:

- Notice when you feel sad.
- Look out for feelings of depression, hopelessness, anger, frustration, or hate. These emotions are often secondary to sadness. Track these emotions and thoughts to the source of the sad emotion.
- Connect to your true self using the True-Self Breath.
- Allow yourself to feel sad. Make peace with the sensations—it is normal! It is your mind's way of releasing the pain of the situation. Respect it for trying to help. (If you feel like crying, allow it.) If your situation is a situation that is from your past, allow yourself to grieve it out.
- Let go of any conditioned egoic thoughts such as: *This sucks. I hate this. Why did this happen to me? It's so bad. It's not fair. It shouldn't be like this.* Thank your mind and recognize the thoughts as your mind's attempt to soothe the sadness.
- Practice self-love exercises of self-care, self-appreciation, appreciation, self-encouragement, and self-compassion.
- Find or create some lighter thoughts.
- Ask yourself: Does it feel true to me to fix this situation, or allow it to be exactly how it is right now?
- Decide how it feels true to you to live despite sadness. Do things that make you feel content or at peace.

Proud or Pleased/Disappointed

Disappointment is a natural reaction when we have not met an expectation we have for ourselves, if a person does not meet our expectation for them, or if we do not get what we want. Just as disappointment is the emotion of unmet expectations, feeling pleased with or proud of oneself is the emotion a person would normally feel if they were to meet or even excel beyond an expectation.

So, why do we experience disappointment? Wouldn't life be easier without it? Just imagine, for a moment, life without disappointment. Aiming for a goal you cannot achieve, but always repeating the same behaviors to achieve it. With this type of action, you would never get anywhere. You would keep repeating the mistakes and never change or adapt the actions to try to improve on what you had previously done. It is here that disappointment can be a great ally. When you feel physical sensations of heaviness of disappointment after not achieving a desired outcome or getting what you wanted, this causes you to stop what it is you are doing. During the pause, your mind will likely reflect upon what you have done or what went "wrong." As you attempt to understand it, you can find ways to improve your future actions. So, disappointment causes us enough pain to try to reinforce positive changes in our behavior for the future. Just as feeling proud or pleased upon achieving an outcome reinforces continuing behaviors or actions which are working well.

Problems with disappointment can arise for three main reasons. The first way in which disappointment can create problems is when disappointment is triggered by high, perfectionist, unrealistic, unhealthy expectations. As these expectations are so high, they are going to be difficult to achieve and thus make us more prone to feeling disappointment than other people with more realistic or healthy expectations.

No amount of learning from mistakes will be able to assist anyone with these expectations in changing their behaviors to perform better in a more balanced and healthy way, as the standard was too high in the first place. Thus, attempting to use disappointment to learn in this experience would likely be detrimental to anyone as there is no lesson to be learned. These expectations are also the types which can result in a denial of feeling proud or pleased with oneself, as the expectation is to achieve such lofty standards, and any meeting them is deemed as normal and thus does not trigger the proud feelings within the person.

The second reason is that disappointment can easily arise within us when we make unavoidable mistakes. Mistakes by their nature are not intentional, and while they can provide a good opportunity to learn, no matter how much we do learn or analyze what went wrong we are still going to make them in the future. In other words, learning from mistakes will not always prevent them from being made. Human beings are fallible creatures after all. Trying to use the tool of disappointment to learn from mistakes that were unavoidable, or where you already know better, only serves to overly criticize us, thus making us feel even more disappointed in ourselves.

Another issue with disappointment is that it is designed as a teacher to help us reflect on what went wrong and try to learn from it. Unfortunately many of us attempt to teach ourselves and learn in an unhealthy, self-hating way. Often people use self-critical, self-punitive types of behaviors to try to teach themselves instead of using kind, compassionate, encouraging, and forgiving words and behaviors of the true self. The more we teach ourselves through self-hate and self-criticism, the worse we are going to feel within the disappointment.

When it comes to disappointment there is no avoiding it. If you have an expectation of yourself, another person, or life (no matter how realistic or unrealistic it may be) you are going to feel disappointed whenever it does not get met. But remember the disappointment is trying to teach you something; it is trying to get you to stop and look into how you can do better next time. Whether it serves our true self to do so is never guaranteed, so try to be comfortable with disappointment without always needing to learn something. Be kind to yourself while you do this. There is no amount of anger, self-hatred, or self-criticism that is going to change the fact that you feel disappointment. When you are okay with disappointment, you engage fully, take worthwhile risks, and behave in ways that give you a chance to succeed and make the most out of your life.

Here are some other emotions with similar functions to disappointment/disappointed:

- dejected
- let down
- upset at myself
- like a failure

Here are some other emotions with similar functions to proud/pleased:

- successful
- pleased with myself
- accomplished

Creating an aligned pathway to deal with disappointment:

- Notice when you feel disappointment.
- Look out for feelings of depression, anger, frustration, hate, self-loathing, lower self-worth. These emotions are

often secondary to disappointment. Track these emotions and thoughts back to the disappointment emotion.

- Connect to your true self using the techniques already discussed.
- Allow yourself to feel disappointed; make peace with the sensations. It is normal for you to feel it when things do not work out how you wanted them to.
- Let go of any disappointment emotional egoic thoughts such as: *I'm terrible. I'm such a failure. I should have done it better. I should never have done it like that. It shouldn't be like this. If only I had done it better. What's wrong with me?* Thank your mind for trying to teach you but it may not be necessary right now.
- Practice self-compassion, self-respect, self-acceptance, self-encouragement, self-forgiveness, and forgiveness to help get through it more easily.
- Find or create some lighter thoughts.
- Once you have made peace with disappointment, use the tool of disappointment. Ask yourself: Is there anything that feels true for me to learn in this situation for the next time? If there is, learn it in a kind way. If not, then there is no need to use the tool of disappointment.
- Decide to live your life as fully and richly as possible, according to your truth. Yes, you feel disappointed, but do the things that are important to you and keep trying and hoping for more.

Clear Conscience/Guilt

The emotion of guilt arises when our behaviors are not aligned with our expectations of how we think we should treat ourselves or others. Guilt can feel like a sickness or heaviness in the pit of your stomach about your actions toward others or yourself. Guilt can assist our true self by setting a standard of acceptable behavior toward others or ourselves. Feeling a clear conscience or at ease with your actions is the opposite of feeling guilty and is telling us we are okay with the standards of behaviors we have engaged in.

Without guilt we would have no guide or beacon for what appropriate and inappropriate behavior toward ourselves or others is. Guilt tends to occur when we have not lived up to what we have learned is the right or wrong way to have treated another or ourselves. Thus, expectation is the cornerstone of guilt. Guilt can also be closely linked with the empathy one is capable of feeling. Those who are extremely empathetic tend to have high levels of guilt and will thus modify their behavior drastically to minimize their "hurtful" impact upon others. Those with low levels of empathy are less prone to feeling guilt and will thus have less of a guide for how to treat others and therefore possibly be more hurtful to them to attain whatever it is they want.

Imbalanced guilt occurs when we excessively put the needs of others in front of our own (we habitually value others over ourselves), when our standards for ourselves are unhealthy, or we excessively put our needs above the needs of others (we only value ourselves and never others). Therefore, guilt causes us enough pain to help us stop to reflect upon our actions in order to minimize their effects on ourselves or other people for future scenarios and stick to a code of conduct more aligned with our true self.

Problems arise with guilt, like disappointment when the standards of how we should treat others or ourselves are either too high or too low. If we have learned that it is more important to give others what *they* want than it is to get what *we* want, then we will be more inclined to feel excessively guilty when it comes to doing something for ourselves. Also, if the standards of behavior we have learned to live up to are too high, then this will also make us more prone to feeling guilty as we will have a hard time achieving such lofty expectations and thus constantly be feeling guilty about not having done what is "good." Having low expectations of our ability to give others what they want over what we want forms a different type of imbalance. It creates the behavior of extreme selfishness and can leave a trail of hurt toward others as we will not be able to take their feelings into account at all when deciding what we do.

Another time guilt can take us further away from our true self is when we do believe the guilt is valid—in that we have truly decided we have done something we believe is wrong. On its own this is not the problem, but rather how we treat ourselves and talk to ourselves when we believe we have done "wrong." Many people can have a tendency to treat themselves critically or hatefully and never forgive themselves for what they did wrong, thus only further reinforcing their guilt feelings.

When it comes to guilt, it is important to examine yourself to see where you lie on the spectrum. Are you someone who feels excessive amounts of guilt no matter what your behavior may be? Or are you a person who only cares about yourself and does not care about others at all, treats everyone poorly, and is disconnected from your guilt feelings? Either way can be imbalanced and wreak havoc in either your life or the lives of those around you, as well as disconnect you from your truth.

If you feel guilty about something you have done, then stop to see what your true self says about expectations you hold for yourself. On the other hand, if people are often upset with you, it may help to examine how your true self wants you to treat others. The guilt (or lack thereof) is helping you live by a standard of behavior. By understanding this you will be able to use the guilt as a guide to assist you in knowing what actions you feel are in alignment with your true self. So, with guilt, like disappointment, listen and learn from past actions and behaviors and forgive yourself while you do this. There is no amount of anger, self-hatred, or self-criticism that is going to change the fact that you feel guilty about your actions.

Here are some other emotions with similar functions to guilt:

- sorry
- regretful
- remorseful
- repentant

Here are some other emotions with similar functions to a clear conscience:

- innocent
- dignified

Creating an aligned pathway to deal with guilt:

- Notice when you feel guilty.
- Look out for feelings of depression, anger, frustration, hate, self-loathing, lower self-worth. These emotions are often secondary to guilt. Track these emotions and thoughts to the source: the guilt emotion.
- Connect to your true self using the techniques already discussed.
- Allow yourself to feel guilty; make peace with the sensations. It is normal to feel it. It is just your mind's way of trying to treat yourself or others better the next time. Thank it for trying to help. (If you feel like crying, allow it.)
- Let go of any guilt conditioned egoic thoughts such as: *I'm terrible. I'm such a failure. I should have done it better. I*

should never have done it. It shouldn't be like this. If only I had done it better. What's wrong with me? I deserve to be punished. Thank your mind for trying to assist, and recognize the thoughts as your egoic self's attempt to learn and get rid of your guilt.

- Practice self-compassion, self-respect, self-acceptance, acceptance, self-encouragement, and self-forgiveness to help get through it more easily.
- Find or create some lighter thoughts. Redefine your moral code to one that is balanced, healthy, flexible and aligned with your true self.
- Once you have made peace with the guilt, sit in your inner truth and ask yourself: Do I truly feel that I did something wrong in this situation? If yes, you can ask: Acting according to my truth, what would I like to do differently next time? If no, continue making peace with guilt.
- Decide to live your life as fully and richly as possible, according to your truth. Yes, you feel guilty, but do the things that are important to you.

Connected/Lonely

Loneliness is an emotion we have when we feel disconnected from those around us. We may feel we have no support, no common ground with anyone, and feel like we are going through our life alone. Loneliness is more than a state of mind; it affects us physically too. Loneliness can feel like a huge void or ache in our heart or possibly in the pit of our stomach. Resisting the void/ache then increases our body's arousal level as it views loneliness as a threat and is thus attempting to motivate action within us to do something to minimize the loneliness. It motivates us toward trying to connect to others. Feeling connected is the flip side to feeling lonely. Loneliness prompts us to attempt to form connections.

As human beings, we are by nature social animals. Evolutionarily speaking, having a social network meant higher levels of support to achieve the daily aspects of living. This in turn led to a higher chance of survival. In essence, being connected to those in our village or tribe was a way to ensure we had enough support around us and enough collective skills to ensure our survival. In order for the social aspect to work, everyone in the village/tribe had their roles to play; thus, hunter and gatherer societies developed. In each role, it served the people to be able to connect to each other in order to function more smoothly and to develop bonds of trust which would serve them for their survival. It also served them to share similar belief patterns, ideologies, and goals that best served the village as a whole. Being connected particularly to the other sex also increased our chances of mating, thus having offspring, and also increased the chances of the survival of the offspring as we had the support to care for them. Consequently, this created a deep connection within the tribe and thus humans evolved with the feeling and deep urge to feel connected with each other.

The emotion of loneliness thus created a longing to help us chase these connections in our life, for as part of a group we feel safer, more secure and connected, and as a couple we have a higher chance of ensuring our own and/or genetic survival.

Most of us tend to gravitate toward people who share our beliefs and values, as well as those with personalities that complement our own. We seek them out because we want to feel connected, understood, loved, and/or accepted by them. This is a normal human behavior and is what loneliness motivates us toward. Loneliness can create enough emotional pain to push us to seek out others and form meaningful or even life-sustaining connections with them.

Problems can arise when we over-rely on the lonely feelings to seek connectedness, or when we must get rid of loneliness at all costs. One reason for this is that in our society feeling lonely and being disconnected from people is not as life-threatening as it once was. In today's society most of us have jobs which provide us with money to meet our basic needs, such as food and shelter. We may also have a social welfare system which can assist us if we are unable to do it for ourselves. In other words, we no longer need to overly rely upon our connections to the "village" for our survival. This does not stop the feeling of loneliness from occurring, but seeking connections under these circumstances is no longer a necessity.

Another reason why attempting to get rid of loneliness does not work is that it is not always possible to connect to others when we want to or as fast as we want to. There is not always going to be someone around to connect with when loneliness arises and it takes time to form connections. Also, seeking to get rid of loneliness at all costs can come across as desperate to the other person, pushing them away and thus reinforcing loneliness.

Another reason why chasing a feeling of connection can be problematic is that it is impossible to fully connect with another person on every level. We are all individuals, and while we may share many similarities, we are not going to overlap perfectly.

When it comes to loneliness, it is important to determine whether trying to get rid of the loneliness serves your true self. Is connection to people a matter of survival? Are you resisting loneliness so much that you have become desperate for any companionship? Is it possible to create a connection as quickly as you would like it? Are you looking for a 100% compatible connection? If your true self is trying to get you to utilize loneliness, act upon it: go out (or online) and seek the connections to make your life richer and fuller. If the loneliness is not facilitating the creation of these connections at the present moment, then allow it to be there. No amount of desperate seeking will solve the loneliness. Your true self wants you to connect to yourself, learn to enjoy your own company, and be comfortable as you are, at least in this moment.

Here are some other emotions with similar functions to loneliness:

- isolated
- alone
- disconnected

Here are some other emotions with similar functions to connected:

- part of
- supported

Creating an aligned pathway to deal with loneliness:

- Notice when you feel lonely.
- Pay attention to feelings of depression, anger, hopelessness, frustration, or jealousy. These emotions are often secondary to loneliness. Track these emotions and thoughts back to the lonely emotion.
- Connect to your true self using the techniques already discussed.
- Allow yourself to feel lonely; make peace with the sensations. It is normal to feel it. It is just your mind's way of motivating you to connect to others. Thank it for trying to help get you connections. (If you feel like crying, allow it.)

- Let go of any loneliness egoic thoughts such as: *When will I find someone? I wish I could have a person in my life who understands me. Why does everyone else have someone? I'll be alone forever. It's not fair. It shouldn't be like this. What's wrong with me?* Thank your mind, and recognize the thoughts as your mind's attempt to soothe the loneliness.
- Practice self-love techniques of self-appreciation, appreciation, self-acceptance, acceptance, self-care, self-compassion, and self-respect.
- Find or create some lighter thoughts.
- Ask yourself: Does it feel true to me to attempt to connect to another person right now? If so, do it. If not, work on your connection to yourself and being comfortable being alone.
- Do something that feels true to you that makes you more content or more connected to yourself or another. Reach out to others; join a group related to your interests; partake in a leisure task solo. This will make the journey through loneliness easier to allow.

Empowered/Powerless

"There is nothing I can do about it" is the most common phrase that accompanies the feeling of powerlessness. Powerlessness comes about when we are unable to control our environment, emotions, or have things be the way we want them to be. When you feel it, you may feel like you can't move your muscles, like you are paralyzed; you may notice tension in different areas of your body; you may feel glued to the chair or floor. These are common sensations people report when powerlessness arises.

Feelings of powerlessness can be useful when utilized in a balanced way. Powerlessness can help us to know when to give up trying or when to let go of things which are out of our control. Imagine for a moment if we did not have the emotion of powerlessness, enough discomfort to make us stop and contemplate our ability to influence events. We would keep fighting and trying to control everything. We would try to control all aspects of our environment and ourselves, even when it was unhealthy to do so and we did not have the ability to control them. Imagine you had a terminally ill parent and had exhausted all treatment options. Continuing to fight and search might create more suffering in you in what could be your last days with your parent. Always trying to fight and control what happens in the world will eventually lead to suffering.

While powerlessness can assist us in deciding when to give up or quit, it can also be useful to motivate us to chase or control our feelings of empowerment, which sit opposite to powerlessness. Having a resistance to powerlessness will give us enough discomfort to keep us motivated to improve or fix whatever the situation may be. It motivates us to take control and try to make things better. Imagine if the women's rights movement had only surrendered to their feelings of powerlessness. Would there be the level of equality there is today? Or imagine your boss was treating you poorly. Feeling powerless could help you to stop and contemplate what action you can take to rectify the situation and retake control.

Powerlessness and feelings of empowerment are flip sides of one emotion. Problems arise within these emotions when we try to avoid one or hold on to the other at all costs. Some people overuse their feelings of powerlessness to the point of surrendering their power and becoming victims of life. They feel like they cannot control anything in their world and give up, allowing life to happen without enforcing any direct influence. Surrendering to powerlessness and giving away control is a way of trying to feel like they are *in control*.

On the other hand, there are people who try to get rid of feelings of powerlessness at all costs. They attempt to control most things within their environment, all the things going on around them, the people they encounter; they try to make everything work exactly how they think it should be working. In essence they are so avoidant of feelings of powerlessness that they will do almost anything and everything to get rid of it or avoid it, even if it is detrimental to them. Everyone will have many versions of ways they try to gain feelings of power and control.

In a balanced true-self way, feelings of powerlessness can help us to surrender when fighting is not necessary, to keep trying to improve things when we have some influence, and to take back control when it serves us. If we are too sensitive to the feeling of powerlessness, we will not be able to utilize it in a balanced way and will be more likely to suffer at some point when the powerlessness cannot be used as designed. Being okay with the powerlessness but also resistant enough to know how/when your true self wants to change things and not become a victim is the best way to utilize the tool of powerlessness.

Here are some other emotions with similar functions to powerlessness:

- helpless
- stuck
- incapable
- losing control
- paralyzed
- oppressed
- controlled

Here are some other emotions with similar functions to empowered:

- in control
- free
- unstuck
- powerful

As you create an aligned pathway to deal with powerlessness:

- Notice you feel powerless.
- Look out for feelings of frustration. Frustration almost always comes secondary to powerlessness. Track this emotion and thoughts back to the helplessness emotion.
- Connect to your true self using the techniques already discussed.
- Allow yourself to feel the powerlessness; make peace with the sensations. It is normal to feel it. It is just your mind's way of trying to get you to either change something or stop trying to change something. Thank it for trying to help.
- Let go of any powerlessness egoic thoughts such as: *There must be something I can do. It shouldn't be like this. How can I fix this? It's not fair. Why me?* Thank your mind and recognize the thoughts as your mind's attempt to get rid of your helplessness.
- Practice self-love strategies of self-compassion, self-acceptance, acceptance, self-appreciation, appreciation, and self-care.
- Find or create some lighter thoughts.
- Ask yourself: Does it feel true to me to do something to improve this situation right now? If the answer is yes, fix

what you can. If the answer is no, recognize that it is okay to feel powerless and allow the situation to be as it is.

- Keep trying to live your life as fully and richly as possible. Yes, you feel powerless, but how do you truly want to live? Focus on the areas of your life where you do feel you have some level of control.

Satisfied/Dissatisfied

Feeling unfulfilled or dissatisfied is the internal sense that something is missing. It may feel like it is missing from your life, or perhaps from you as a person. It may be like a void within, or hollowness in parts of your body. Feeling unfulfilled can be a great motivator to assist in searching for fulfillment, in searching for what it is that makes us feel satisfied.

Satisfaction often arises when we attain what it is we were searching for. Thus, feeling dissatisfied could help our true self to stop and think about what we believe we are lacking or want, and help us stay motivated enough to continue searching and working toward attaining it. As an emotion, then, it is a useful tool to assist and motivate the search, to discover what is important to you and your life. This then not only helps us achieve our goals, but more importantly for our mind and body it relieves us of any dissatisfaction or sense of feeling unfulfilled (at least temporarily). Perhaps it helps to motivate us to get a better job, or maybe to eat better or to get more fit. Maybe feeling unfulfilled will help us learn when to move house or leave a relationship.

While finding what it is we want can lead to satisfaction, problems can arise because no sense of satisfaction lasts forever. The sense of fulfillment will be temporary, as our mind will then move on to the next thing it feels we need to help us to feel fulfilled. Problems arise again when we chase away feelings of dissatisfaction for feelings of fulfillment or satisfaction no matter the cost. So, in a sense, problems occur when we feel we "need" something for satisfaction rather than "want" something.

Attempting to chase fulfillment will definitely take us out of the present moment. It will always keep us future-focused and not focused on or engaging in life now. The problem arises because we cannot enjoy or savor what we have; we are unable to stop and smell the roses, so to speak. It can also take us away from acceptance of what is going on right now, or who we are right now. Attempting to only feel satisfied will lead to searching and chasing. This will then, in turn, lead to a huge sense of dissatisfaction and also a sense of fatigue and tiredness as the searching does not allow for rest. It may also lead to a sense of self-hatred or hatred as we can only feel satisfied with ourselves or life when we attain the "perfection" we seek.

Another problem of constantly chasing away the sense of feeling unfulfilled is that these feelings may be cyclical. In a job, in a relationship, who has not felt unfulfilled or dissatisfied at some stage? It is a normal response when we have experienced the same thing for a period of time. If we had to act upon every sense of dissatisfaction we had, we would never last within a relationship or a job (or anything else for that matter) for long.

The true self always feels fulfilled right now—although it may trigger the emotion of dissatisfaction to help motivate action toward something even more fulfilling. When you do feel unfulfilled it is important to assess and examine what it is you want and why you want it. Do you want something so you can feel better about yourself? Do you want it so others will like you? Do you feel you need it rather than want it? If your motivations for feeling satisfied are only about filling emotional voids then, while you will feel better in the short term, you are almost guaranteed that these feelings will return in the longer term. This is not what our true self wants for us. But if you embrace yourself or what it is you have right now, and still feel dissatisfied, and you have looked at what emotional voids you are attempting to fill, then perhaps it is time to reflect on what you want and to search for that could increase your level of satisfaction.

Here are some other emotions with similar functions to dissatisfaction:

- empty
- hollow
- unfulfilled
- unappeased
- insatiable
- bored
- directionless

Here are some other emotions with similar functions to satisfaction:

- fulfilled
- appeased
- satiated
- interested
- complete
- directed

Creating an aligned pathway to deal with dissatisfaction:

- Notice when you feel dissatisfied.
- Look out for feelings of sadness, hate, helplessness. These are common emotions secondary to dissatisfaction. Track these emotions and thoughts back to the dissatisfied emotion.
- Connect to your true self using any of the techniques discussed.

- Allow yourself to feel the dissatisfaction; make peace with the sensations. It is normal to feel it. It is just your mind's way of trying to get you out of the moment and make you search for more for yourself. Thank it for trying to help.
- Let go of any dissatisfied egoic thoughts such as: *When I have [ABC] then I'll feel better. I'll be happy when ABC happens. Everything will be better when I get ABC. Why can't I have it? When will I get it?* Thank your mind and recognize the thoughts as your mind's currently unnecessary attempt to get rid of your dissatisfied feelings.
- Use self-love tools of self-compassion, self-appreciation, appreciation, self-acceptance, acceptance, self-encouragement, possibly even bravery.
- Find or create some lighter thoughts.
- Ask yourself: Does it feel true to me to move toward something more right now? If yes, work toward it. If not, make peace with the feeling of dissatisfaction.
- Keep trying to live your life as fully as possible. Yes, you feel dissatisfied, but what is it in you or in your life that makes you feel fulfilled? (Our minds are good at focusing on what we don't have rather than what we possess.) Focus on your areas of contentment. Start with smaller things and gradually build up as you become more awake to yourself. Create a list of things you may like to try to add to your life.

***

The happy/sad family of emotions is mostly about our relationship within ourselves and the environment. The pleased/hurt family is more about the relationship we have with others and their treatment of us.

Chapter Thirteen

The Pleased/Hurt Family of Emotions

Pleased/Hurt

Hurt is the emotion that gets triggered within us when we think we have been poorly treated by another person. When it occurs, we may feel emotional pain within us. The pain is often reported within the chest or heart area and physically aches for many people. Just as we may feel hurt by others, we may also feel pleased by the actions of others. This is the opposite emotion to hurt, feeling pleased or feeling "good." Pleased often manifests as tingling and lightness within the body. This is the emotion we want, right? To feel good and nice whenever someone acts toward us and never feel hurt. It is impossible to feel pleased without knowing hurt. How could a person know they felt pleased if they did not know how it felt to be hurt? Both emotions are at relative points to each other.

But why can't we just have pleasurable feelings?

To understand the answer, it may help to imagine a life without the feeling of hurt. Think about how you might allow people to treat you if you did not feel hurt emotions. Would you have any impetus to set limits or boundaries with people, or would you let them do what they want to you, despite whatever negative impacts it might be having on your life? The feeling of hurt is the emotion that says to us we do not like how we are being treated and we do not want to continue dealing with it. The dislike of hurt can be our true self asking us to speak up and say: "Stop," "Enough is enough," "I won't take this anymore." Hurt is attempting to protect us from mistreatment and to set limits with the other person in regard to what behaviors we will or will not tolerate from them.

Hurt within society or a community can help us decide which people to keep close and which to keep at a distance. We are more likely to want to be near those who cause the least amount of hurt and to keep those who cause the most at a distance.

Problems with hurt arise for numerous reasons. One such reason is if the hurt standards of behavior or expectations of others are set too high. If they are too high, then you are going to be highly prone to feeling hurt by everyone around you. You will go about your life feeling that only a few people treat you well and the others are plain mean or nasty people. This would normally result in many relationships or friendships that are turbulent, or that end often and badly. In other words, the people cannot deliver the standard you require and thus you or they either end the relationship or continue to fight or argue over the "hurt" caused to you. Problems can also occur for the opposite reason—when expectations are too low. Perhaps you were treated poorly as a child, so you continue to expect such treatment as it feels familiar. People like this are so used to being hurt that they do not advocate for themselves and set limits for how they wish to be treated—which then leads them to be continuously poorly treated and hurt.

Other issues with hurt occur when people do not recognize the emotion as hurt. In fact, most of the time when we feel hurt we go automatically into anger, as anger is usually the means by which we set limits to protect ourselves from further hurt. If people do not recognize the hurt under the anger, then they are left trying to deal with the wrong emotion and thus not knowing the most effective way to react or speak. People can also do the opposite and go into anxiety to self-advocate when hurt, or even into numbness, and thus are not or may not be aware that they feel hurt at all.

Other issues with hurt arise as part of living life. We are going to feel hurt eventually—though people are not always going to hurt us intentionally, and even if they do, there may not be the opportunity or need to set a limit with the person every time the hurt arises. Reacting to hurt with anger in these cases can create further issues within the interpersonal relationships you have.

To live a life with others and to be able to feel the pleasurable or good feelings from how we are treated, we must be willing to allow for and accept a level of hurt in our lives. We do not share the same agreement for standards of treatment of each other. We are also prone to acting and hurting others out of our own emotional responses. This then guarantees that at some point in our life we will not only feel hurt by another, but will also hurt someone else, if not ourselves. We want to be okay with this feeling. Our true self may want us to set limits with another person in order to establish how we would like to be treated, or it might want us to move on and forgive. Ideally, if setting limits, we can set them in a way most aligned with our true self at any given moment.

Here are some other emotions with similar functions to hurt:

- betrayed
- disrespected
- violated
- used
- offended
- unfairly treated
- victimized

Here are some other emotions with similar functions to pleased:

- treated well
- respected
- fairly treated

- valued
- pampered
- pleasured

Creating an aligned pathway to deal with hurt:

- Notice when you feel hurt.
- Look out for feelings of anger, frustration, resentment, numbness, hate, despair, anxiety, unworthiness. These emotions are often secondary to hurt. Track these emotions and thoughts back to the hurt emotion.
- Connect to your true self using the techniques already discussed.
- Allow yourself to feel hurt; make peace with the sensations. It is normal to feel it. It is just your mind's way of helping you to decide how you want to be treated. Respect it for trying to help.
- Let go of any hurt egoic thoughts such as: *I hate this. They should not treat me like that. They are wrong. It's not fair. It shouldn't be like this. Why are they behaving like this? I don't care.* Thank your mind, and recognize the thoughts as your mind's attempt to soothe the hurt.
- Practice self-love skills of forgiveness, self-compassion, compassion, self-acceptance, acceptance, self-advocacy, self-appreciation, and possibly bravery.
- Find or create some lighter thoughts.
- Ask yourself: Do I feel it is true to me to set a limit with this person in this situation? If the answer is yes, do it in the truest way of self-advocating possible for you. If not, allow the hurt to be there.
- Continue living your life and do something that makes you feel better or pleases you. This will make the journey through hurt a little easier to work with.

Accepted/Rejected

Most of us have heard the expression "It does not matter what people think of you." If this statement was so true, we would not feel such a large sense of rejection when other people disapprove of us or dislike us. Rejection is the function of not belonging or being accepted as you are. It usually manifests as pain in our heart or emptiness in our gut. It is a feeling which can arise when a person does not like, accept, or approve of us.

The reason we feel so much pain at being rejected is that the sense of rejection has served us as humans for many years. Feelings of belonging and being accepted are primary functions within humans which aid in creating a sense of community and safety. The sense of community was extremely important when our ancestors lived as parts of tribes or villages. In the past, being part of the community was necessary for our survival. Being rejected by the village meant having to live an isolated life, which would have been more life-threatening to us. Without the emotion of rejection we as humans would not have modified our behaviors to fall into line with the "crowd's ideals," thus guaranteeing a higher chance of our survival. Without the community, our life was in jeopardy, therefore rejection helped us change ourselves to conform with the important people around us. Being part of the village was safer than being an outsider.

Rejection makes us stop to reflect upon ourselves and our actions in order to assist us in determining whether it would serve us to change how we behave to increase our chances of belonging or receiving acceptance from others. Thus, giving up part of ourselves and our individuality can help ensure our acceptance as part of the community.

Being rejected in today's society is mostly no longer life-threatening. We are less likely to be killed or to starve if we are not part of a group or wider community. Rejection now serves more as a tool to assist us in seeking the approval or acceptance of others. Feeling rejected now makes us think about ourselves and our actions and contemplate whether they are "appropriate" and allow us to be accepted or liked by others. This can help us grow and learn how to treat people better.

While a common sense of agreed-upon behaviors can assist us as well as a community (such as laws or rules), it can also disconnect us from our true self when we seek the approval of others at the expense of being one's true self and valuing self-acceptance over that of others. Constantly seeking the approval of others without knowing what feels right for us can create difficulties in knowing ourselves and knowing what it is we believe, prefer, or like. Instead, we are too often focused on what we think the other person/people will like and can lose our connection to ourselves for the sake of their conditional acceptance. This also means we must tamp down or suppress our true nature.

Problems can also arise when other people have conflicting ideas of what it is they would like from you. Not everyone is going to like the same things, so pleasing everyone is impossible. Thus, avoiding rejection is not possible.

We live in a world with so many different personalities, different appearances, different beliefs, different cultures, and different opinions about right or wrong, acceptable or unacceptable. A world with over 8 billion people will have no uniform idea of what is deemed acceptable or not when it comes to avoiding a sense of rejection. Feeling rejection is guaranteed at some point. Are you willing to stand strong within your true self and can you love yourself enough to be okay not to be accepted by everyone (especially those you want acceptance from)? Can you reflect upon your behaviors and adapt without losing yourself? Can you accept yourself when others do not? Your true self can and does.

Here are some other emotions with similar functions to rejected:

- disapproved of
- disliked
- unloved
- embarrassed
- excluded
- hated
- outcast
- invalidated

Here are some other emotions with similar functions to accepted:

- approved of
- loved
- liked
- included
- understood
- validated
- admired

Creating an aligned pathway to deal with feelings of rejection:

- Notice when you feel rejected.
- Look out for feelings of anger, anxiety, resentment, low self-worth, or hate. These emotions can be secondary to rejection. Track these emotions and thoughts back to the rejected emotion.
- Connect to your true self using the techniques already discussed.
- Allow yourself to feel rejected; make peace with the sensations. It is normal to feel it. It is your mind's way of

getting you to stop and think if you should change your behaviors. Thank it for trying to help.

- Let go of any rejection egoic thoughts such as: *What's wrong with me? I need to be better. I need to fix [such and such] about me. How could they not like me? Why don't they like me? How dare they? How am I going to cope if they don't like me?* Thank your mind and recognize the thoughts as your egoic mind's attempt to soothe the rejected feelings and find ways to be approved of.
- Practice self-acceptance, self-appreciation, self-compassion, self-respect, self-encouragement, and bravery.
- Find or create some lighter thoughts.
- Check in with yourself and ask: Does it feel true to me to modify my behavior in this situation, or to be accepting of who I am without changing anything?
- Live life from a place of liking and accepting yourself. Remember you are an individual. It is okay to not fit in; it is okay to not be liked by everyone. Work on accepting yourself, because your true self-opinion matters most.

Received/Abandoned

The emotion of abandonment is one closely related to rejection. Abandonment will normally arise within us when we have been left or neglected by someone we care about. It will normally create the physical response of a sense of emptiness within. Experiencing abandonment is used as a tool to motivate us to seek the "safety" of the crowd. Knowing the feeling of abandonment is also what assists us in knowing what it is like to be received by another person. It helps us understand when we are welcomed within a group. Abandonment is like rejection but differs in that with rejection a person sends the other person away from them; with abandonment the person is the one who removes themselves from the unwanted person.

In the past, abandonment by our peers or social group almost always meant death, due to the difficulties of functioning alone. Thus, the fear and pain of abandonment motivated us to search for another group to receive us or to again seek the approval of our own group. The sense of abandonment arose to help us to gravitate toward the safety of a group. Total isolation in the past would have meant certain death. Today it may assist us in conforming to keep a job or to change behaviors in relationships. It helps us follow social norms and cues, which can assist in making society run more smoothly.

While a useful tool to encourage conformity, problems with abandonment can also arise. One such issue can occur with people who have experienced large abandonment in their lives (particularly in childhood). These people, as teens/adults, are sensitive to any behavior perceived as abandonment by others and often find it difficult to trust. As a result of their past abandonments, they believe people will not love or receive them and will therefore eventually abandon or leave them. This can result in the person testing their loved ones with poor treatment and behavior to see if they will stay around. Almost all people have some level of patience and tolerance, but most of us will eventually reach our limit with these bad behaviors and end up leaving or abandoning the person. While fortunate for the person who leaves, the beliefs about being abandoned by everyone only then become reinforced in that person.

Other issues with abandonment can occur when conformity to the desires of the individual or masses may go against our inner truth. We must sacrifice too much of ourselves to be received by others, who are often only responding to their own fears of abandonment. This will often result in much anxiety and a sense of dissatisfaction within relationships and within oneself. It can also result in a disconnect from our truest desires and wants.

Another issue with abandonment is that living without the group is no longer so life-threatening. We can go about our lives without much assistance from others if required. We are able to sustain our physiological needs in a more solitary life which once would have killed us.

Not everyone we encounter will remain in our lives forever. Different people will play different roles in our lives and for different time periods. Sometimes this means you may be abandoned by another person, but perhaps it means you are the one doing the abandoning. It is bound to happen at some point. People can grow apart; people can change; people's needs change. We are all not going to welcome each other, and sometimes the best way of dealing with the person is to walk away or abandon them. The more we recognize abandonment as a possibility of life, and know how, whether, or when to utilize it to change or not, the more chance we have of building real meaningful relationships that the true self is capable of.

Here are some other emotions with similar functions to abandoned:

- deserted
- unwanted
- dumped
- neglected

Here are some other emotions with similar functions to received:

- welcomed
- nurtured
- wanted
- remembered

Creating an aligned pathway to deal with feelings of abandonment:

- Notice when you feel abandoned.
- Look out for feelings of anger, resentment, anxiety, low self-worth, or hate. These emotions can be secondary to abandonment. Track these emotions and thoughts back to the abandoned emotion.
- Connect to your true self using the techniques already discussed.
- Allow yourself to feel abandoned; make peace with the sensations. It is normal to feel this. It is your mind's way of motivating you toward returning to the safety of the group. Thank it for trying to help.
- Let go of any abandoned egoic thoughts such as: *What's wrong with me? I need to be better. I need to fix [such and such] about me. I can't live without them. I can't do this alone.* Thank your mind and recognize the thoughts as your mind's attempt to soothe the abandoned feelings and find ways to be received by others.
- Practice self-acceptance, self-appreciation, self-compassion, self-respect, and self-encouragement.
- Find or create some lighter thoughts.
- Check in with yourself and ask: Does it feel true to me to modify my behaviors in this situation in order to be welcomed, or to be accepting of who I am without changing anything?
- Receive yourself and do something that is nice for you. Remember that you are a unique individual. You are able to cope. Although having the support of other people might be your preference, it is not necessary. Some people

> will stick with you and others will not. Some people may be in your life for a reason, a season, or a lifetime. Welcome and receive yourself and you will be set free.

***

Whereas hurt is very much connected to our relationship with others, there is a set of emotions completely connected to the relationship we have with ourselves.

Chapter Fourteen

The Relationship-with-Self Family of Emotions

Worthy/Unworthy

Feeling good about ourselves and worthy as a person is something most of us desire. None of us like it when we feel low self-worth or unworthy. We turn inward and feel small or not good enough. Physically we may feel constricted as if we are shrinking, or perhaps we have a sinking feeling within our heart or stomach. Feelings of low self-worth will plague us at some stage in our lives. Feeling not good enough is designed to motivate us to chase and strive to get better at things or improve, so we can feel good enough or worthy.

When we are children, we are taught which qualities or situations are better and which ones are worse. Depending on which of these we do or do not possess, we then interpret our sense of worth from it. The more we possess, the higher our sense of worth; the less we possess, the lower our sense of worth. It also means, though, that our self-worth and feeling good enough becomes conditional upon those qualities.

Self-worth is a piggybacking emotion. That is, it will accompany many of the other emotions (particularly: guilt, disappointment, rejection, disapproval, abandonment, and hurt) when they occur. The reason being that it stems from the mind functioning we have as children. As children we are egocentric—we believe the world revolves around ourselves and everything that happens is a reflection of us. When we partake in a particular behavior, we generally receive approval or disapproval from those around us (particularly our parents, peers, society, school). The approval/disapproval takes the form of labeling the child, such as telling the child they are bad or naughty, or perhaps smart or pretty. If we receive approval, we feel worthy; if we receive disapproval then we feel there must be something wrong with us or we are unworthy. So, we engage in the opposite behavior so we can be validated by a parent or caregiver in order for us to feel worthy, or just believe we are unworthy as we are.

A sense of self-worth is also derived from beliefs of the world where value judgments are made about traits, qualities, achievements, behaviors, roles, postcodes, appearance, nationalities. Whenever we are taught that one thing is better than another, we also learn that to possess the opposite is worse and therefore a bad thing. Therefore, if we possess the supposed "bad" thing or do not possess the supposed "good" thing, we feel unworthy or not good enough. When we learn a belief about what makes us worthy, we also learn the belief about what would make us unworthy.

Feelings of low self-worth create two types of behavior, and most of us will engage in both types of behaviors at different times and in different situations. One behavior is more aligned to trying to avoid the feelings of low self-worth at all costs. It involves overdoing things, striving, or chasing the "standards" of what would make the person worthy. The other behavior is normally agreeing that I do not meet those standards and then wallowing in feelings of inadequacy and not trying or striving at all. Both behaviors can be equally problematic in that if we over-strive, we are constantly overdoing things and may burn ourselves out. We may even sacrifice our family, friends, or even our health to meet the "standards" of worthiness. Those of us who do not try, though, also create problems for ourselves. We never achieve anything important to us because we do not feel we are good enough, which then results in perpetuating our feelings of low self-worth.

Overall, chasing self-worth by chasing/chasing away beliefs of better/worse is a futile exercise. The best we can do with it is to subdue it for a short period of time before it occurs again. The reason for this is there is no criterion that defines our worth as a person. No real standard exists of what traits, qualities, achievements, behaviors, intelligence, roles, postcodes, appearance, nationalities are better or worse. These are only belief patterns passed from one person to the next, then further perpetuated by certain parts of society agreeing with these beliefs and praising those who share them, or ignoring, shunning, or even attacking those who don't. In reality we are worthy exactly as we are. We do not need to be more or have more of anything to be worthy. We are born worthy and do not need more or less of anything to be more than that. Feeling lower and higher worth are just relative points to us being worthy as we are within the wholeness of our being.

The one time our true self will utilize feeling less worthy or not good enough is if it feels it can help us to recognize areas in ourselves or our lives where we can improve and/or grow. It is important to remember that even if you improve on an area, it does not make you more worthy. It is about improving on an area because it is valuable or aligned to you, not because you wish to eliminate the feelings of low worth.

Other names for emotions similar to unworthy:

- not good enough
- less than
- inferior
- inadequate
- small
- dumb
- deficient

Other names for emotions similar to worthy:

- good enough
- more than
- superior
- equal to
- smart
- complete
- competent

Creating an aligned pathway to deal with unworthiness:

- Notice when you feel low worth (which often piggybacks onto the hurt, rejection, abandonment, guilt, and disappointment emotions).
- Look out for feelings of anger, self-hate, jealousy. These emotions are often secondary to low worth. Track these emotions and thoughts to the unworthy emotion.
- Connect to your true self using the techniques already discussed.
- Allow yourself to feel unworthy; make peace with the sensations. It is normal to feel it. It is just your mind's way of helping you to try to improve on something, whether you need to or not. Respect it for trying to help.
- Let go of any low-worth egoic thoughts such as: *I must not be good enough. I'm only adequate if or when [such and such]. I'm such an idiot. How could I have been so stupid?* Thank your mind and recognize the thoughts as your mind's attempt to get you to chase feeling more worthy.
- Practice skills of self-acceptance, self-appreciation, self-respect, self-compassion, and self-encouragement.
- Find or create some lighter thoughts.

- Check in with yourself: Do I truly need to improve in this area, or am I good enough as I am?
- Ask yourself: What would I do if I felt worthy already? Then proceed and live your life as fully as possible.

Self-Love/Shame

Shame is the feeling we have when we want to hide from embarrassment, guilt or other shadow emotions. And never be seen again. It is the sense of wanting to pull our heads deep into our necks and disappear forever. Shame feels like a sinking feeling within us. We want to become smaller and hide so that others are not able to see us. We get down on ourselves and hate ourselves for what we have done or how we are, and have high hopes the people around us are not aware of our behaviors and supposed flaws. The opposite of shame is the feeling of self-loving or self-acceptance; feeling we are fine just as we are and do not need to hide or change anything about ourselves.

Shame is an emotion that is a combination of emotions. It usually has a combination of the emotions of low worth or inadequacy, embarrassment, self-rejection, disappointment, guilt, and self-hate. When these emotions occur, shame results, as we severely criticize ourselves and put ourselves down about the situation, behaviors, thoughts, emotions, or traits we possess or which relate to us.

Shame is a learned emotion and comes from the lessons and beliefs regarding right and wrong as well as good and bad about us as a person. These beliefs are derived from family, school, society, or media depictions of what is acceptable and what is not acceptable to possess as a human being. Therefore, shame will only occur when having done, said, or possessed something we have learned to judge as undesirable, bad, or wrong.

The use of shame is that it can help us to hide the deepest parts of us. This can be useful to gain acceptance from others and, from an evolutionary perspective (as mentioned previously), to survive, as we still remain part of the greater group if we do not display or show undesirable qualities or behaviors. It can also be a benefit to assist us in suppressing certain traits and qualities within us that may not serve us in a situation. Feeling the shame can help us learn not to repeat the behavior again in the future and therefore teach us about how we do and do not want to behave as a person.

Shame can be extremely problematic too. Every single one of us has positive and negative qualities and behaviors about us. These qualities have the ability to serve us at one point or another. Overusing shame to suppress these qualities means that if we do need to use them, then we will not have access to them as we deny them in ourselves or try to avoid using them. Thus, we may not be able to appropriately react to the situation with what is required, and not allow our truest nature to reflect the situation. For example, shame about laziness would force me to suppress it, then overwork more often than is healthy, thus leading to burnout.

Shame can also be problematic when the standard of behaviors we have learned for ourselves is too high. We then spend much time hiding, avoiding, or denying those aspects of ourselves, and we do not allow ourselves to be free to be ourselves. Shame also requires us to hate ourselves, which leads us to further cycles of suffering and discomfort with who we are. Shame also means we must hide ourselves for much of the time so we can fit in. This then creates a false sense of what it means to be human and then perpetuates the beliefs in those around us that these qualities are indeed bad. This creates a façade we live in that makes us feel disconnected from those around us.

Shame when used against a behavior or quality can sometimes be of assistance if done with self-love and care, as it can hide a trait or quality which may not be useful at that moment of time or in that situation. If overused, shame can be a self-destructive emotion which will absolutely hinder our ability to live as our truest selves. It will force us to hide every single quality, trait, or thought, and live our lives as an idea of what we should be, not the complete person we truly are. If shame is helping you to recognize certain traits that might not be useful, use it to possibly change your action in that moment. If not, it would serve you to change your beliefs regarding what you need to feel ashamed about and give yourself the freedom to accept, display, or discuss your qualities. Also use shame as an opportunity to grow your acceptance of whatever you feel shame about. Shame will disappear when you bring the object of your shame to light and accept it within yourself.

Other names for emotions similar to shame:

- ashamed
- self-rejection
- self-disgust
- self-hate
- self-anger
- self-disapproval
- self-dislike

Other names for emotions like self-loving:

- self-accepting
- self-appreciating
- self-liking
- self-approving
- self-content
- at peace with self
- self-owning

Creating an aligned pathway to deal with shame:

- Notice when you feel shame (shame often comes with or as feelings of low worth or inadequacy, embarrassment, self-rejection, disappointment, guilt, and self-hate).
- Allow yourself to feel the shame; make peace with the sensations. It is normal for it to be there. It is your mind's way of attempting to help you to hide something you learned was bad. Thank it for trying to help.
- Connect to your true self using the techniques already discussed.
- Let go of any shame egoic thoughts such as: *I am bad for having this. It is wrong for me to feel or think this way. I shouldn't be like this.* Thank your mind and recognize the thoughts as your mind's attempt to get you to change so you can accept yourself.
- Practice skills of self-acceptance, self-appreciation, self-respect, self-forgiveness, and self-compassion. You might not like the quality or behavior, but you do not need to hate yourself for possessing it.
- Find or create some lighter thoughts.
- Ask yourself: Does it feel true to me to push this behavior or attribute away for this situation, or to utilize it to assist me? Do which one feels true.
- Own yourself as you are and live your life as freely and truly to you as possible, despite the shame you feel.

Secure/Vulnerable

Among all the emotions we attempt to control, feeling vulnerable is high on the list of the most avoided. A good majority of our defense strategies have been designed to minimize our vulnerability and thus protect us from not only physical, but mostly emotional pain. Being vulnerable is how we entered the world. We were at the mercy of our environment, and if it was unkind to us, we would definitely have not survived.

Thankfully as babies we had not yet developed a sense of self and were unaware of our vulnerability. As time went on, we became increasingly aware of ourselves as a body that felt physical pain and as a conscious person who experienced emotional pain. In our interactions with our environment we began to get a sense of what could be harmful or threatening and thus made us feel vulnerable, and what made us feel safe or secure. Feeling secure and safe are the opposite sides to vulnerability.

When we were children, we experienced the world with unguarded openness. From there, each one of us experienced our initial pain both physically and emotionally and have thus developed a belief system around what it is that may harm us and what it is we deem as safe. In turn, this leads us to develop feelings of vulnerability which can make us behave carefully and be wary so as to avoid further pain. Most of us go into a state of defensiveness to protect ourselves and to feel secure from perceived threats. For this we go into the "fight, flight, or freeze" mode (more on this later) as it is our protector designed to help save us from physical or psychological harm.

Vulnerability can assist us, though. One such way is that it provides a warning sign for us that there may be a possible threat lurking. In doing so, vulnerability then triggers within us our defense mechanisms designed to either prevent the threat from occurring or prepare for ways to manage the threat if it were to occur. For example, if a person has previously put me down for wearing my hair a certain way, I may feel vulnerable when putting it in the same style. The vulnerability is attempting to warn me a threat is possible due to the past experience of being put down. Vulnerability also helps us by triggering the "fight, flight, or freeze" response to assist us in acting more quickly should the actual threat be a physical one like being in a dangerous situation.

Problems with vulnerability can occur when we overuse it and want to feel safe or invulnerable at all costs. In turn, this leads us to feel anxious, then to fight or flee when a threat has been perceived, or to be angry and have anger outbursts once a perceived threat has already taken place. Avoiding any vulnerability can be limiting to our lives. It does not allow for experiences to occur and relationships to develop. Not allowing vulnerability means we cannot try anything new as it may be deemed as physically or emotionally threatening. It also means we must live guardedly and distrust everyone and everything around us, leaving us feeling isolated and most likely dissatisfied with our lives.

Overall, vulnerability when used effectively can be a great ally in protecting us from physical and psychological pain. It can be extremely limiting to our lives if we must avoid risk at all costs. Allowing room for the possibility of emotional and physical pain can lead to a much more fulfilling and content life overall, and help build loving and supportive relationships around us and within ourselves. It will assist in creating experiences that align with the desires of our truest self. When we have the ability to accept any emotional discomfort, pain, or even death into our lives, this sets us free to be able to truly live our lives from our heart's deepest desires and gives us a sense of invulnerability or true strength.

Other names of emotions similar to vulnerable:

- weak
- exposed

- sensitive
- open
- insecure
- susceptible
- unsafe

Other names of emotions like secure:

- safe
- strong
- insusceptible
- protected
- stable

Creating an aligned pathway to deal with vulnerability:

- Notice when you feel vulnerable (vulnerability often arises when you perceive someone or something as threatening).
- Look out for feelings of anxiety or anger. These emotions are often secondary to vulnerability. Track these emotions and thoughts to the vulnerable emotion.
- Connect to your true self using the techniques already discussed.
- Allow yourself to feel vulnerable; make peace with the sensations. It is normal to feel it. It is just your mind's way of helping to protect you from perceived threat. Thank it for trying to help.
- Look out for any emotional worry thoughts that will nearly always accompany vulnerability. *What ifs...?* or predictions. Thank your mind and recognize the thoughts as your mind's attempt to protect you from possible harm.

Notice what emotions your mind is trying to protect you from. Practice allowing those emotions.

- Practice self-love skills of self-acceptance, self-trust, self-encouragement; surrender and utilize your courage.
- Find or create some lighter thoughts.
- Ask yourself: Does it feel true for me to try to protect myself from this perceived threat or to allow the feeling of vulnerability?
- Ask yourself: Am I willing to allow myself to be vulnerable in this situation so as to truly live the life I want to live? If so, surrender to what may be and have courage and take the chance to live.

***

Our relationship-with-self emotions revolve around the conditioned egoic self and are designed to motivate us to survive or improve. The one thing all the primary emotions have in common is that they exist to motivate action and changing of our behaviors and/or thoughts. This change, however, is usually created by using different intensities of the resistance emotions.

Resistance emotions are ones our true self can use to protect us from danger and motivate us to control whatever primary emotions we may be having within a situation. The reason being that when we feel bad enough, the resistance emotions will kick in to push us toward attempting to change or cope with the situation we are in. While helpful at times to assist us in living as our true self, they can also cause us problems if used solely from the point of our conditioned egoic mind. The resistance emotions come under the anxious, anger, and freeze families of emotions.

Chapter Fifteen

The Relaxed/Anxious Family of Emotions

Relaxed/Anxious

Anxiety is the emotion we have which is responsible for keeping us safe and assisting us with improving our chances of survival. Traditionally, when we are faced with a danger it triggers within us the "fight, flight, or freeze" response. The "fight, flight, or freeze" response results in numerous changes within the body designed to increase our chances of survival. When the threat to us has passed, our body will slowly return to a state of relaxation as it no longer needs to protect us.

Just imagine walking into a forest a thousand years ago to forage or hunt for food. As we walk about the forest, we see a wolf there in the distance. Our mind has been taught and therefore conditioned to know we are in a vulnerable state and the situation is potentially a dangerous, life-or-death one. So, to enhance our chances of survival, our body goes through numerous changes. These changes are part of the "fight, flight, or freeze" response and each symptom is specifically designed to increase our chances of surviving this encounter.

These symptoms include: our mind becoming focused; vision narrowing; increased breathing rate; increased heart rate; increased sweating; dry mouth; slowing of the digestive system; increased muscle tension; blood diverting away from the hands, feet, and head; slowing of the immune system; and the adrenal glands releasing adrenalin.

Each symptom has a use to assist in our survival:

- mind becoming focused: occurs due to the mind only requiring the attention and functioning to view the danger and to formulate a plan away from the danger

- vision narrowing: occurs to minimize any distractions or unnecessary information which may impede escape
- increased breathing rate: occurs to fill the body with oxygen to fuel the movement of the muscles
- increased heart rate: occurs to pump the oxygen to the muscles necessary for fighting or fleeing
- increased sweating: occurs to keep the body cool during the incident
- dry mouth; slowing of the digestive system: The digestive system slows down to conserve energy not required for survival. Saliva is the first line of the digestive system, therefore it slows down accordingly.
- increased muscle tension: occurs to prevent injury in the fighting or fleeing
- blood diverting away from the hands, feet, and head: occurs as blood is diverted to more necessary organs/ muscles required for survival
- slowing of the immune system: also occurs as a means of conserving energy not required for survival
- adrenal glands releasing adrenalin: occurs to give the body a boost of energy that may assist in saving our life.

Overall, the purpose of anxiety is to save our lives. Imagine our life without anxiety, without the alarm system to help us to fight or flee when danger presents itself. Few of us would still be alive today without anxiety to assist us in navigating the sometimes-dangerous world. If our anxiety is due to a life-threatening situation, then it would serve us to use it to save our lives. Run or fight or freeze—do what is required to survive.

If our anxiety occurs without the presence of danger, then we need to dig a bit deeper for the cause. To understand this type of anxiety, it is important to understand the functioning of the human mind on a deeper level. The human mind learns from any events we have ever witnessed, whether in real life, in the media, or even simply described by others. If these past events appear to the mind to be situations where our life may have been at risk or in danger, then the mind stores the information for something to remember as being dangerous should it occur the next time around. To return to the wolf analogy, if I had been able to escape the wolf the first time but had to return to the same forest the next week, I would most likely find myself feeling anxious at the prospect of entering the forest again even if the wolf was nowhere to be seen. Because of my past experience, my mind perceives the forest as a dangerous place where a wolf could attack and possibly kill me at any moment. The anxiety is not triggered by actual danger, but rather by the perception or anticipation of danger. In other words, if we believe something to be a threat it will trigger anxiety within our body.

The purpose of this type of anxiety is to help us be prepared for any possible danger that lurks. By being overly cautious about danger it prepares our body to react quickly should danger present itself. Consequentially our response time becomes quicker, thus again more greatly increasing our chances of survival. If we have this type of anxiety, it is a good idea to use it if it keeps us alert and aware enough to minimize danger or risk. If not, we must examine what we believe is dangerous. Perhaps the thing we fear is not as dangerous as we believe, or maybe we are over-estimating the chances of the threat. It may also be important to examine whether it is worth taking the risk of facing the danger to give us the life we truly want. The supposed safety of avoidance or constant vigilance may come at a huge cost to our life and our truest desires.

Our human needs evolved over time, and the emotional situations which were dangerous to us in the past no longer pose the same threat. For example, in the past the isolation of loneliness would have been life-threatening, whereas nowadays it is rarely so dire. So, anxiety did not only occur when actual danger was present, or if we believed a situation to be dangerous; anxiety also arose when there was a psychological or emotional threat to us, when there was a possibility of a bad outcome that created emotional pain. A bad outcome can be defined as a situation which triggers unpleasant (or shadow) emotions. If we did not feel unpleasant in the situation it would be a neutral outcome, or if we felt pleasant we would deem it as being a good outcome.

The purpose of this type of anxiety is to assist us in preventing bad outcomes from occurring. In fact, having some level of anxiety during certain tasks can assist us in our performance and thus makes us more likely to succeed and minimize having shadow emotions about the outcome. This form of anxiety is the most common for many people today. Centuries ago, we lived in a world where threats and potential danger were far more constant. Now we mostly live in a world where our main threats are emotional and/or psychological. The threat comes from events which make us feel "bad" emotionally, such as feeling sad or vulnerable if I were to lose my house, or feeling embarrassed if misspeaking in front of a group.

This type of anxiety can be useful for us as humans. By having some anxiety about an event, our performance levels can increase and thus our chances of experiencing a bad outcome can decrease. Problems here can arise when the anxiety level is too high, which occurs when we have learned an exaggerated sense of how bad the outcome is or when our sensitivity to the possible emotion is amplified. We have thus developed a higher level of avoidance and aversion to the primary emotion that would arise in the situation. For example, a person who has been regularly and harshly criticized for making mistakes as a child would likely suffer from anxiety in situations where disapproval may arise. Thus, they would likely suffer from severe anxiety during a task where there is a chance of them making mistakes in front of others. The anxiety is attempting to prevent the feeling of disapproval from arising in the person by making them vigilant about the possible bad outcome during the event.

Unfortunately, when it is excessive it usually keeps us hyper-aware, thus negatively impacting our performance levels. If the anxiety level for a task you are facing is at a moderate level where it does not interfere with your performance, then thank it for doing its job. It is attempting to help you get your desired outcome and avoid a bad one. If the anxiety seems too high for the situation, it would be important to investigate what emotion the anxiety is trying to prevent.

Anxiety primarily attempts to prevent emotions in the sad, hurt, and relationship-with-self family of emotions. If this is the case for you, then spend some extra time learning about those emotions and ways to deal with them. Make peace with the anxiety and the emotions it is trying to prevent for you. Allow the sensations of them to be there in your body. Thank the anxiety for attempting to prevent the other emotions, but its assistance is not needed this time around, or perhaps it is not needed to the degree it is there. Remember, the anxiety is only trying to heighten your abilities and performance levels to protect you from the chance of feeling "bad."

Here are some other emotions with similar functions to anxiety/anxious:

- afraid
- panicky
- scared
- fearful

Here are some other emotions with similar functions to relaxed:

- calm
- at ease
- peaceful

Anxiety as an emotion can come at differing levels. Generally speaking, there are lower levels on the anxiety scale that come out before full-blown anxiety. Anxiety itself will occur when you are in a life-threatening situation, in a perceived life-threatening situation, or in the process of partaking in an activity or facing a situation which you have learned to fear.

Uncertainty or stress/pressure usually arise before full-blown anxiety. If you are anxious about something that is not life-threatening, it is highly likely that you have gone into anxiety as a means of attempting to control your uncertainty or stress/pressure.

Creating an aligned pathway to deal with anxiety:

- Notice when you feel anxious.
- Look out for and write down egoic thoughts such as: *What if...? I wish I knew. If only I could get the answer.* Add any other questions or worries that have no answers.
- Allow yourself to feel anxious; make peace with the sensations. It is normal to feel it. It is your mind's way of trying to protect you from being physically or emotionally harmed. Thank it for trying to help.
- Connect to your true self using the techniques already discussed.
- Think about your worries and ask yourself what emotion you would have if the worry were to eventuate. Allow the possibility for those emotions to be there too; make peace

with them. Remember, though, it is the thoughts that are creating the emotion, not the current reality, as the worry has not come true.

- Surrender to the possibility of your worries coming true once you have faced them. Thank your mind and recognize the worry as your mind's attempt to protect you from something it may not be able to prevent. If it is going to happen, then so be it. Anxiety and worry will not stop it.
- Use self-trust and courage to help enact your decision.
- Find or create some lighter thoughts.
- Ask yourself: What course of action, if any, feels true to me in this situation? Does it feel true to fight, flee, avoid, face, or stay in this situation?
- Live your life as fully as you possibly can despite feeling anxious. Trust yourself to manage with whatever emotions may occur for however life may turn out.

Certainty/Uncertainty

Uncertainty is an often-overlooked emotion within us as humans. Uncertainty usually arises on two occasions. One of those occasions is when we do not have an answer to a situation. The other is when we do not know the outcome of a possible future event. In order for uncertainty to arise under these two conditions, the situation we feel uncertain about must be of relevance or importance to us, that is, it is a situation that could trigger an undesired shadow emotion. The situation we feel uncertain about is one where we think there is a chance of a bad outcome. So, feeling the emotion of uncertainty about whether it will rain tomorrow is not likely for me, but if tomorrow happens to be a day where I planned a lovely picnic where I was going to propose to my girlfriend, then I'm sure I am going to feel a lot of uncertainty about not only the weather but also what answer she will give me. The reason being that the disappointment level would be higher if it rained or she said "No." The opposite emotion to uncertainty is certainty, and this emotion taps into our sense of safety and security. When we feel certainty it brings a sense of calm and relief to our body and mind. When we feel uncertain we normally have a sense of tension and heightened awareness within our body and mind. It is the tension which is most useful for us when uncertainty works as it is designed. The purpose of uncertainty is to assist us in preparing should a dangerous or bad scenario arise. When we have uncertainty our body tenses, our awareness is heightened, and we remain on the lookout for any possible threat. Uncertainty can work by helping us to plan, prepare, search for answers, or predict the future in the name of preventing a bad outcome. For example, imagine a person suffering from severe abdominal pain. They feel uncertain about what is causing the pain. Their dislike of the uncertainty may motivate them to visit their doctor to find an answer. This might in turn lead to them getting an answer and therefore feeling certain and ideally preventing a "bad outcome."

It is the emotion of uncertainty which motivates us to seek certainty. Imagine for a moment a life without feelings of uncertainty. Life without uncertainty seems nice, until we look deeper, that is. Without uncertainty we have nothing to prompt us to prepare for any possible danger, no emotion to assist us in being prepared should we need to react, nothing to motivate us to create Plan B or predict possible outcomes, no emotion to assist us in mitigating risk, or to help us prepare for what may occur, every situation coming as a complete shock. Doesn't seem so nice, does it? In fact, without uncertainty there is a high chance many of us would not be alive today. If we were alive, we would be living a pretty risky life in terms of danger and also in terms of more regularly experiencing undesired outcomes. It is the feeling of uncertainty that assists us in preventing some of the bad outcomes. So, we can hopefully see by now, uncertainty can be a useful tool for survival and minimizing negative outcomes.

Problems arise with uncertainty when we try to seek certainty when it is not available, or when we try to get answers for future situations we cannot possibly know—for absolute certainty about a situation is only something we can get with time. There are only two certainties: death and change. The rest is possibility or probability. Only time can tell us if or when a situation will arise, and only time will give us the answer to some problems. No matter how much I research, I am still not going to know for certain what the weather will be like tomorrow, and I definitely will not know for certain if my girlfriend is going to say "yes" to my proposal. When trying to solve uncertainty does not work, it would serve us to surrender to whatever may occur, wait, and see. Most of us have much difficulty with surrender and a wait-and-see approach. We do not like to give up our control; we do not want to wait and see. We want answers now; we want to know what is going to happen. In other words, we want to feel certain now. Because we want to feel certain now, our mind will send us worry thoughts to try to find an answer or predict what could occur. My mind would ask: *What if she says "no"? What if it rains? What am I going to do? What if she rejects me?* Uncertainty triggers worried thoughts like asking *What if...?* to guess outcomes, and leads us to try to predict things, mind-read, Google for answers, ask people their opinions, research statistics, remind ourselves of probabilities, check the weather forecasts (repeatedly!), and engage in a whole array of behaviors to find out for certain what is going to happen. What ends up happening is that we amp ourselves up into a more intense state of anxiety because we cannot get certainty. Then the more anxious we feel, the more inclined we are to worry, and the more we worry, the more anxious we feel. We get stuck in a loop of worry and anxiety, yet our mind only worries because it is trying to resolve uncertainty.

But what if it is okay to feel uncertain? What if you surrendered to whatever it is you are worrying about? What if you allowed yourself to feel the tension of uncertainty without guessing or predicting an outcome? What if you made the decision to wait and see, instead of trying to prepare for something you can obviously not fully prepare for? What if you took a chance, even though you did not know how things would turn out? What if you decided to trust yourself to cope with whatever the outcome might be? Do you think the uncertainty would trigger extreme anxiety before the situation? The answer is no. When you allow yourself to feel uncertain and surrender to whatever may be, yes you still remain at the heightened state of awareness of uncertainty and fear, but the anxiety will be lower or will not come until the event occurs, if at all.

Another way to deal with uncertainty is to write down what your worries are. While the uncertainty is trying to prevent these worries from coming true, it is trying to prevent you from suffering from a "negative" emotional reaction should the worry eventuate. The uncertainty is trying to help prevent me from feeling sad and rejected from a "no" answer to my proposal. If I am okay to feel sad, disappointed, and rejected at the thought of a "no," then my sensitivity to the particular worry will decrease. The way to become desensitized to a worry is to allow the emotion attached to that worry to exist within you. Make peace with it like you would with the uncertain feelings. The good part about uncertainty is your worries have not yet come true, so you need only face *a thought* of a bad outcome, not the bad outcome itself.

Here are some other emotions with similar functions to uncertainty:

- nervous
- uneasy
- unsure
- doubtful
- confused
- suspicious

Here are some other emotions with similar functions to certainty:

- confident
- at ease
- trusting
- relieved
- having clarity
- assured

Creating an aligned pathway to deal with uncertainty:

- Notice when you feel uncertain. Look out for and write down thoughts such as: *What if...? I wish I knew. If only I could get the answer.* Or notice when you are asking questions that have no answers.
- Look out for feelings of anxiety, frustration, or anger. These emotions are often secondary to uncertainty. Track these emotions and thoughts back to the uncertainty emotion.
- Connect to your true self using the techniques already discussed.
- Allow yourself to feel uncertain; make peace with the sensations. It is normal to feel it. It is your mind's way of trying to get answers or to prepare for something it may not be able to prepare for this time. Thank it for trying to help.

- Notice that the uncertainty is attempting to prepare you for a possible bad outcome.
- Surrender to the possibility of your worries coming true once you have faced them. Thank your mind and recognize the worry as your mind's attempt to prepare for something it may not be able to prepare for. If it is going to happen, then so be it. Uncertainty and worry will not stop it.
- Use self-trust, self-encouragement, and courage to assist you in making your decisions in this time of uncertainty.
- Find or create some lighter thoughts.
- Ask yourself: Does it feel true to try and get certainty right now, or does it feel true to wait and see what happens?
- Wait and see if or when the time comes. Live your life as fully as you possibly can despite feeling uncertain, and trust things will turn out as they will, and you have the ability to cope with whatever may occur.

Ease/Pressure

"I'm stressed" is a common saying going around these days, at least in my experience. Most people report feeling large amounts of stress or pressure going about their daily lives. Whether it be financial, work, family, health, or time constraints, pressure will play a large part in our lives. Pressure is our body's way of responding to any kind of real or imagined expectation. When an expectation (internally or externally) is placed upon us, our fight-or-flight system will kick in to pressure us to respond to the demand. Experiencing pressure is part of being a human and it can motivate us toward action that helps to avoid unwanted outcomes and get wanted outcomes. Pressure is always caused by the expectations we place upon ourselves. Although we may feel it when expectations are placed upon us by others, this does not cause the pressure. Only if we accept their expectations does it impact on us as pressure. The expectations we place upon ourselves come from the "should" thoughts, in that they motivate and pressure us to do certain behaviors.

Pressure is designed in our bodies as a way to assist us in avoiding "bad" outcomes that may make us feel unpleasant. To push us toward what we truly want, which would then make us feel pleasant. Putting pressure on ourselves to do or achieve certain things can assist us in trying harder to prevent unwanted consequences and achieve wanted consequences, which is unwanted or wanted emotional consequences. Having a certain level of pressure can increase our performance levels and thus help us to achieve better results with the things we pursue, making us feel more pleasant and avoiding the unpleasant feelings. Having low or no levels of pressure can result in a complete lack of motivation and also no desire to achieve or do anything. While it is a useful state to be in at times, it would not assist us in living a rich, full, true life. Imagine feeling no pressure to pay your mortgage or having no fear of losing your job; you would spend money wherever you wished or only turn up to work whenever you felt like it. Both scenarios would likely result in you having no money to support your lifestyle, and possibly no home to live in. Having a sense of expectation to go to work today will generate pressure within us to push us to go to work and prevent the bad outcome of sadness or loss of security in the face of homelessness. The expectation is helping us to avoid losing our job and feeling sad and loss of security.

Problems with pressure are not uncommon. Most of us live our lives according to these expectations and do not stop to question whether they go along with what we truly want. We do not ask: Are these expectations healthy or sustainable for me? In a sense we can become slaves to our habitual expectations and thus become disconnected from what we truly want in favor of trying to get things for the sake of avoiding an emotion. We live a life under a self-dictatorship which limits or eradicates our freedom of choice, making us feel pressured, overwhelmed, and frequently stressed. Another issue with pressure is that we are doing it in a sense to avoid the unwanted emotional outcomes. If we cannot tolerate the idea of these outcomes, then the pressure levels we subject ourselves to as we avoid or prevent them end up being high and thus our performance levels go down, more likely getting the outcome we are trying to avoid. For example: the thought of failing an important exam causes me to feel so disappointed that I tell myself I must study and do my best. The excessive pressure required to "do my best" can mean I am too highly pressured and then will probably perform worse. If I were to surrender to the thought of failing the exam, my stress levels would come down and I would still be able to study and partake in it, though with a calmer approach. Another issue with pressure is when it becomes relentless; this occurs especially within people who have perfectionist tendencies. Their expectations are so high, they are constantly under stress and pressure to achieve everything their mind tells them to do. This will eventually lead to feeling overwhelmed and anxious, and possible burnout, as our bodies can only take on board so much stress for any period of time.

Symptoms of excessive pressure usually include:

- Feeling overwhelmed and anxious
- Becoming easily agitated, frustrated, and angry
- Having difficulty relaxing
- Low energy
- Headaches
- Upset stomach, including diarrhea, constipation, and nausea
- Aches, pains, and tense muscles

- Insomnia
- Forgetfulness
- Inability to focus
- Difficulties with decision-making

If pressure is helping you to achieve what you truly want in a healthy and balanced way, then utilize those "shoulds" to help motivate you to live the life you want to live. If the pressure is excessive and getting in the way of living the life you want, or is creating problematic symptoms, then it would be important to learn to manage the pressure emotion.

Here are some other emotions with similar functions to pressure:

- stressed
- burdened
- obliged
- overwhelmed
- pressed

Here are some other emotions with similar functions to feeling at ease:

- relaxed
- relieved
- comfortable
- peaceful

Creating an aligned pathway to deal with pressure:

- Notice when you feel pressured.
- Look out for and write down the "should" thoughts and beliefs such as: *I should be, I have to, I need to,* or *I must.*

Look out for feelings of anxiety or being overwhelmed. Track these emotions and thoughts back to the stress and pressure emotion.

- Allow yourself to feel pressure; make peace with the sensations. It is normal to feel it. It is your mind's way of trying to motivate you into action. Thank it for trying to help, but its assistance may not be required.
- Connect to your true self using the techniques already discussed.
- Ask yourself: How would I feel if I did not do whatever the "should" is telling me to do? Allow those emotions to be there too; make peace with them. Remember, though, it is the thoughts that are creating the emotion, not the reality.
- Surrender to any thought of a "bad outcome" or unpleasant emotion your mind might send you. Thank your mind for trying to prevent it, but its help might not be needed so strongly or at all.
- Find or create some lighter thoughts.
- Practice self-compassion, self-trust, courage, self-acceptance, and self-respect.
- Ask yourself: Does it feel true to me to do something in this situation and to what level, or to just allow it to be as it is?
- Do what it is that is important to you. Live as fully as possible despite the pressure you may feel.

***

The anxiety family overall is the family of emotions we use to prevent any unwanted emotions from occurring. If you feel the anxiety emotions it will be useful to ask: *What emotion is the anxiety trying to prevent for me?* When it comes to anger, it is usually the emotion that tries to protect us when we already feel one of the primary emotions and creates a momentum of movement toward something we deem as being better or safer.

Chapter Sixteen

The Calm/Angry Family of Emotions

Calm/Angry

Do these bodily sensations sound familiar?

Your mind becomes focused; eyesight narrows; increased breathing rate; heart pounding blood around the body; increased sweating; dry mouth; slowing of the digestive system; increased muscle tension; blood diverting away from the hands, feet, and head; slowing of the immune system; and the kidneys releasing adrenalin. You'd be forgiven for thinking I was talking about anxiety again, but I'm not, I'm talking about anger—the "fight" to anxiety's "flight."

Anger and anxiety are the primary emotions responsible for keeping us safe and assisting us in improving our chances of survival. When we are faced with a danger, it triggers within us the "fight, flight, or freeze" response. The "fight" response in particular is designed to protect us from the danger and give us extra strength and determination to fight our way out of trouble. The emotion the "fight" uses is anger.

Everyone has felt angry before. From mild aggravation to outright rage. Anger is like our body's bodyguard which protects it from danger or from being injured. In today's society, while it does still occur, it is not overly common for us to require anger to protect us from much physical danger or harm. Most of us get angry about things that are not a threat to our lives, and we react to them as if our lives were in danger. The reason we get angry about things which do not threaten physical harm is because the conditioned egoic mind perceives psychological or emotional threat to self the same way as if there was a physical threat. So, being hurt emotionally would be seen the same as being hurt physically.

This is not all bad. I'd like you to take a moment to imagine living life without anger. Imagine how many people would be able to walk over you. Imagine how difficult it would be to exert your will or desires. Imagine also how difficult it would be to prevent others from hurting you physically or emotionally. These things would not occur without anger.

In these situations, the true self can utilize anger to assist us. Anger can help us to set limits with others; it can help us to exert our will to get our desires or needs met. It is also a helpful motivator to fight against any situation which causes us emotional pain. In other words, having anger can help us get things done or solved, which can lead us to a sense of feeling calm or at ease. Telling people what we do not like in an aligned, firm, or assertive way can assist us in getting our needs met.

Problems with anger are common and they can come from two sides of the coin: those who overuse anger and those who suppress it or do not utilize it as an ally. Let's start with those who overuse anger. Unless you are in physical danger, anger is predominantly a secondary emotion. It generally comes after the primary emotions. What anger attempts to do in these scenarios is to motivate us to set up a protection mode against those people or situations which may be causing or creating the psychological or emotional pain. As an example, if someone takes advantage of me and I feel hurt, getting angry may assist me in setting a limit with them to stop what it is they are doing. By getting angry at them we are attempting to stop the person from engaging in the behavior or stop the situation from continuing to occur in order for us to feel better. This can be done by setting firm boundaries, communicating wants, shouting, screaming, using intimidating or violent behavior, or many other behaviors too. Obviously, a person reacting in some of these ways will have trouble dealing with others as they may bully their way into "protecting" themselves or use the protection methods when unnecessary.

Anger is also inherently connected to our expectations—to the internal rules or codes of conduct that we think not only we, but also the world, should abide by. If anything occurs that goes against these "rules" of right or wrong, anger will often arise to motivate us to enforce what we believe should be the right course of action. While this can sometimes be helpful to get the things "we" want to happen, it is important to remember there are no actual rules for life, and people can do or behave exactly as they desire. Everyone has different expectations and there is no absolute right or wrong in the world. People who have high expectations or rigid beliefs about what "should" occur tend toward excessive anger, and thus excessive exertion of their will. These excessive or rigid expectations can also mean the person is extremely sensitive to any perceived emotional pain and therefore sets excessive limits or boundaries of behavior from others. An example is a person who always gets angry or annoyed at the slightest of grievances.

While utilizing anger can be both useful and problematic, so too can under-utilizing it. The main benefit of not using the anger when it occurs is that it can keep the peace with the person or situation that triggered the anger which gives us a sense of safety and feeling accepted. By not becoming reactive with the anger, we can have the opportunity to choose our behavior more carefully and respond in a way which could be more likely to get our needs met or help us be listened to. If the anger suppression is too extreme, we can easily allow others to take advantage of us and never stand up for ourselves. We do not exert the will of the true self enough and we are always at the mercy of others. An example is a person who is continually spoken to badly, but never says anything out of suppression of their anger. People who bottle up or suppress their anger can reach a stage where they explode at the smallest of things. They can also resort to passive aggressive strategies for getting their needs met. Most people who suppress their anger do so out of a fear of feeling disliked, rejection, or disapproval from others. Others repress their anger due to believing they will not be heard or get their needs met anyway, so there is no point in speaking up.

If anger is assisting you in setting clear limits or preventing bad outcomes from occurring in a healthy balanced way, continue to use it. If it is helping you to attempt to exert your will in a way that does not dominate the other person, then keep going just as you are. If you overuse your anger in ways which steamroll others, or if perhaps you do not use anger enough, then it would be important to listen to your true self and either act upon the anger or make peace with the anger.

Here are some other emotions with similar functions to anger:

- mad
- furious
- irritated
- outraged
- annoyed
- agitated

Here are some other emotions with similar functions to calm:

- peaceful
- at ease
- accepting
- relaxed

Creating an aligned pathway to deal with anger:

- Notice when you feel angry.
- Look out for feelings of sadness, hurt, rejection, embarrassment, guilt, dissatisfaction, disappointment, abandonment (or any other of the primary emotions we have discussed). These emotions are often underneath anger. Track the anger back to the primary emotion(s).
- Once you have understood the primary emotion, utilize the strategies taught in the book to help you cope with them.
- Connect to your true self using the techniques already discussed.
- Allow yourself to feel angry; make peace with the sensations. It is normal to feel it. It is your mind's way of trying to exert your will or expectations, or attempting to protect you. Thank it for trying to help.
- Let go of any anger egoic thoughts such as: *They should not have done that. That is wrong. This shouldn't be happening. It shouldn't be like this. How dare they?* Thoughts of blame are also common with anger. Thank your mind and recognize the thoughts as your mind's attempt to prevent or stop the painful emotion.
- If you are scared to express your anger or dissatisfaction, explore what you are afraid of and what emotions would occur if you did express it. Often the emotion people most fear from expressing anger is in the realm of the rejection/abandoned family.
- Practice self-acceptance, acceptance, appreciation, self-compassion, self-respect, forgiveness and self-forgiveness.
- Find or create some lighter thoughts.

- Ask yourself: Does it feel true to me to exert my will or protect myself in this situation, or to allow it to be as it is? What feels like the truest way to exert your will?
- Move on and live your life as true to you as possible.

Allowing/Frustration

Frustration primarily occurs as a secondary resistance emotion too. That is, it is more of a functional emotion which attempts to solve the emotions occurring prior to it. The primary emotion under frustration will likely be the emotions within the powerless group of emotions. Just as with the powerless family of emotions, though, there is often an accompanying other primary emotion along with it. For example, I may feel powerless about something that makes me sad or dissatisfied. When we feel stuck or powerless, we will trigger frustration, which can work as a motivator to continue trying to change the situation despite the difficulties we are enduring in the situation. The physiological response to frustration is almost always tension of some sort. Different areas in our body will tense up in resistance to the helplessness and thus help motivate us to forge ahead to try to take back the control we so desire.

When frustration is used in alignment with the true self, it can help us stay motivated enough to persevere with the issue and to overcome the sense of powerlessness we feel. Problems occur with frustration when we continue to attempt to control things beyond our control or if we do not take the appropriate action to control the situation. This is when frustration moves into a powerlessness, frustration, powerlessness, frustration cycle. It continues to reinforce a sense of powerlessness, while continued resistance to powerlessness continues to reinforce frustration. It can lead to major anger issues and even depression.

The major antidote to frustration is to allow or make peace with the feelings of powerlessness or lack of control and to grieve what it is you feel powerless about. Once you do so, you may find that you can find a solution to your problem and can solve it, despite the fact that you initially felt powerless. Ongoing frustration can assist in causing enough emotional distress to remind you to reflect upon a situation where a solution may appear at a later time. Or perhaps you may not be making enough peace with feeling powerless and not changing your perceptions about the situation.

Creating an aligned pathway to deal with frustration:

- Notice when you feel frustrated. Look out for what it is you are trying to change.
- Look out for feelings of helplessness and powerlessness. These emotions are always underneath frustration. Track the frustration back to the primary emotion(s).
- Once you have understood the primary emotion, utilize the strategies taught in this book to help you cope with them.
- Connect to your true self using the techniques already discussed.
- Allow yourself to feel frustrated; make peace with the sensations. It is normal to feel it. It is your mind's way of trying to motivate you to change what it is you do not like. Thank it for trying to help.
- Let go of any frustration egoic thoughts such as: *It shouldn't be like this. Why? This shouldn't be happening.* Thank your mind and recognize the thoughts as your mind's attempt to prevent or stop the helplessness.
- Practice self-acceptance, acceptance, self-compassion, self-respect, self encouragement and self-appreciation.

- Find or create some lighter thoughts.
- Ask yourself: Does it feel true to me to resist this powerlessness, or allow the situation to be as it is in this moment?
- Move on and live your life as fully and richly as possible. Yes, you feel frustrated, but do you want to let this take over your whole life?

Embracing/Hate

When we hate something, it is our body/mind's way of helping us to push away or repel that thing and to keep it from being part of our life. Hate normally manifests in the body as tension and it can also have a sense of heaviness attached to it.

Generally, there are two types of hate. The first is where hates derives from a sense of ignorance and fear—based on belief patterns a person has learned that identify something as a potential threat.

Hate in this function is an evolutionary response. By keeping away things we think are different from us and therefore threatening (because we cannot trust them), we can keep ourselves safer. Hence it is a hate born out of fear. This type of hate can be learned, but it may also arise due to our ability to notice differences between ourselves and others. It is based on our learning growing up and what we have been taught to see as "normal" standards. Most examples of this type of hate revolve around discrimination of people or objects, such as certain sexes, genders, sexual orientations, races, religions, personality traits, behaviors, cars (and the list can go on). The opposite emotion to this type of hate is embracing or acceptance.

The problem with this type of hate is that it is generated by ignorance. It is created by the false beliefs that because something is different it cannot be trusted, or it is a danger to us, or it is wrong. These definitions do not exist anywhere but in the mind. "Different from us" does not always mean "threatening." We are not born with concepts of normal or different, better or worse. These are taught to us by those around us and by our lived experiences of "normal." Those around us have usually learned this type of hate out of a response to fear. Racism is a version of this. Many people are taught that one race is superior to another, so they hate the other race. As far as I'm aware, there is no actual magical stone tablet or mystical scroll where this is written, thus making it true. But because it has been so deeply conditioned and because the conditioning creates the hate feeling, continuing to believe it continues to generate the hate inside and thus reinforce the beliefs. This type of hate creates separation between us as people and thus repels us from each other.

The second type of hate occurs when we feel emotional (or physical) pain about something and then, as a secondary emotion, try to push away the pain, reforming it into hate. Hate thus arises out of a desire to resist any other primary emotional or physical pain we may be feeling. Examples are hating someone who has caused you to feel hurt or betrayed, or hating something that makes you experience sadness.

This version of hate is about an attempt to shut out other painful emotions. The hate is a secondary emotion where it is trying to assist us by repelling the perceived object of our pain. It can be as small as hating broccoli as a way to avoid/repel an unpleasant taste, all the way up to hating a religious group due to the pain you feel about how some of its members may have treated you or other people. Hate can be a useful tool to keep people/things away from you which cause you pain. The problem with it, though, is that it is a reactive hate. It is a coping mechanism developed by your mind to try to protect you from emotional pain. If you are not okay to feel the pain, you will be stuck in hate and in a reactive state where you are not addressing the primary emotion.

Hate is a particularly useful emotion as it will indicate how much resistance you have with your emotions at any given moment. One of the main purposes of this book is to show you that you don't need to hate your emotions, but rather you can understand how they can help you. Thus, instead of repelling, bypassing, or stifling our emotions, we can allow them to exist as possible useful tools to help us live our truest life.

Here are some other emotions with similar functions to hate:

- loathe
- detest
- despise
- feel disgust

Here are some other emotions with similar functions to embracing:

- accepting
- being at peace with
- love
- calm
- liking

Creating an aligned pathway to deal with hate:

- Notice when you feel hate.
- Look out for feelings of sadness, hurt, rejection, embarrassment, guilt, disappointment, abandonment, fear (or any other of the primary emotions we have

discussed). These emotions are often underneath hate. Track the hate back to the primary emotion(s).

- Once you have understood the primary emotion(s), utilize the strategies taught in the book to help you cope with them.
- Connect to your true self using the techniques already discussed.
- Allow yourself to feel hate; make peace with the sensations. It is normal to feel it. It is your mind's way of trying to repel things that are causing you pain. Thank it for trying to help.
- Let go of any hate egoic thoughts such as: *It's terrible. That is wrong. This shouldn't be happening. It shouldn't be like this. How dare they?* Thank your mind and recognize the thoughts as your mind's attempt to prevent, resist, or stop the painful emotion.
- Practice self-acceptance, acceptance, self-compassion, compassion, self-respect, self-forgiveness, forgiveness, courage, and surrender.
- Find or create some lighter thoughts.
- Ask yourself: Do I need to repel this feeling of hate? If the answer is yes, allow yourself to feel, but stop and see what the best way to repel it might be. If the answer is no, allow the feelings of pain and hate to be, without trying to control the situation.
- Move on and live your life as fully and richly as possible. Yes, you feel hate, but do you want to let it take over your whole life? Make your decision about what course of action feels true to you in the situation.

At Peace/Resentment

The emotion of resentment is one that will commonly arise out of a combination of sadness, dissatisfaction, hurt, anger, hate, and sometimes jealousy. There are usually two types of resentment. The first is one that comes out of a sense of others getting things you would like, or feeling as if you are giving more than you are willing or wanting to give. The other resentment comes out of being hurt or sad about something, then blaming the hurt or sadness on another person or thing. Resentment usually requires a buildup over time to create it. It often starts as feeling dissatisfied, annoyed or frustrated. Resentment, like most of the anger emotions, will usually manifest in our body as tension and resistance. You may feel a strong sense of wanting to lash out or scream, or you may dwell or ruminate heavily upon the object of the resentment.

In most instances, resentment will occur within a situation in which you believe you have given others what they wanted, but you did not get what you wanted. An example being a person who starts to feel resentful that they are always compromising and giving to their partner and not getting what they want. The resentment will then be directed toward the other person (at least internally, if not externally) and we will become fixated on the fact that the other person got what they wanted, while we missed out. This resentment arises out of a sadness or dissatisfaction about not getting our needs met, usually over a period of time. It is our body's way of telling us we are giving away too much of ourselves and not getting enough in return (perhaps out of guilt, fear of disapproval, or denial of anger). Waiting for the other person to give us what we want is not going to be enough to get rid of the resentment. First, we must understand what it is we do want, more so than what it is we do not want. Second, we must realize that mostly, no one can take from us unless we decide to give to them. If we are resentful about not receiving what it is we would like, it is our responsibility to get it. It is our responsibility to decide what we want and to attempt to make it happen—either by asking for it, or by giving it to ourselves. If resentment has set in, it is most commonly caused by us not taking responsibility for our choices and also not having spoken up earlier about situations we do not like. Because we did not speak up, others might have thought we were at peace with what was happening and had no motivation to change anything or give us more.

The second type of resentment comes from a deep sense of sadness or perceived hurt that was "caused" by another person or thing. We blame a person if they hurt us, and we internalize anger and hatred toward them. As this blame grows, we cling to the resentment. It is often easier for us to hold on to resentment (anger and hate) than it is to sit with the pain we feel about what we believe is happening or has happened to us. Holding on to the resentment gives us a sense of power over the "culprit" who has caused or is causing us pain. Holding on to resentment also means we suffer, and the power is not real. We hold on to the tension, and we also hold on to the pain within us.

To deal with this type of resentment we must be willing to feel the pain, work at forgiving the person who caused the pain, and then take responsibility for our life moving forward. Only forgiveness and taking responsibility will release us from the resentment. When we blame a thing (such as the universe, the government, or "life") for our emotional pain, resentment will also arise. It arises this time from a sense of being a victim to a person, life, or God. The longer we hold on to blame, the longer we continue to be a victim of life's woes and thus continue to hold on to resentment about our life. To get through this type of resentment we must take responsibility for improving or creating our life. We must recognize that our life is our responsibility and only by grieving our pain and taking control will it ever change or be improved. If we continue to hold on to a victim mentality about the sadness or emotional pain in our life, we will continue to reinforce any pain we are already suffering from and fuel resentment. While being a victim can help reduce some responsibility, overdoing it keeps us feeling like a victim and thus we continue to feel victimized by life or others.

Here are some other emotions with similar functions to resentment:

- bitter
- spiteful
- ill-willed

Here are some other emotions with similar functions to being at peace:

- calm
- peaceful
- at ease
- accepting
- relaxed

Creating an aligned pathway to deal with resentment:

- Notice when you feel resentful. Look to see which type it is. Are you feeling sad about not getting what you want, or is it more about you feeling hurt by someone or something?
- Look out for feelings of sadness, hurt, rejection, fear, dissatisfaction, low self-worth, abandonment (or any other of the emotions we have discussed). These emotions are often underneath resentment. Track the resentment back to the primary emotion(s). Also be on the lookout for anger; it often comes when you have a buildup of resentment.

- Once you have understood the primary emotion(s) connected to resentment, utilize the strategies taught in the book to help you cope with them.
- Connect to your true self using the techniques already discussed.
- Allow yourself to feel resentment; make peace with the sensations. It is normal to feel it. It is your mind's way of trying to prevent sadness or feeling hurt. Respect it for trying to help.
- Let go of any resentment egoic thoughts such as: *It's their fault. How dare they? F*** them.* Thank your mind and recognize the thoughts as your mind's attempt to prevent or stop the painful emotions.
- Practice self-acceptance, acceptance, self-appreciation, appreciation, self-care, self-compassion, self-respect, self-forgiveness, forgiveness, and courage.
- Find or create some lighter thoughts.
- Ask yourself: What do I want from this person? Am I willing to take responsibility for creating or asking for what it is I want? Am I willing to forgive the person for the pain they have caused me? It is okay to feel hurt, but am I going to choose to live my life fully despite what is happening or has happened?
- Move on and live your life as fully and richly as possible. Yes, you feel resentful, sad, or hurt, but do you want to let it take over your whole life? Decide what feels true for you to do in the situation.

Compersion/Jealousy

I want it! Why do they have it and not me? How dare she talk to that other man! Do these thoughts sound familiar? If so, there is a high chance you have been bitten by the green-eyed monster. That's right! You are feeling jealousy—that tension which attempts to prevent you from losing your relationship or that makes you extremely aware of what it is you do not have. Compersion is the opposite of jealousy. It is being at ease with, peaceful about, or even happy for others having what they have. Jealousy is also a secondary emotion, and it functions for two distinct reasons, the first being a fear of hurt or loss, and the second as an external deflection mode of dealing with one's own sadness or low self-worth.

Let's start with the first type. Evolutionarily speaking, jealousy is an emotion which assisted us in attempts to guarantee our parental lineage and protection. On the male side, being jealous of a partner would be enough to attempt to control their behaviors so as to guarantee that the child she may be bearing was his and not some other man's. On the female side, being jealous of a partner would be an attempt to control him in order to prevent him from fathering other children with other women and thus being unable to dedicate his time, energy, and resources to her or their children, which would result in a lower survival rate. In other words, jealousy attempted to assist a person in controlling their partner for the purpose of guaranteed preservation of their genetic line and/or the higher chance of survival which two parents (instead of one) offered. Jealousy has therefore been an extremely useful emotional tool to further propel humanity forward in relation to survival and population growth.

The emotion of fear underlies both of these versions of jealousy. In both instances it is the fear of being unable to guarantee a genetic lineage; for the male, the genetic lineage and offspring survival are the issues, whereas for the female, it's about her own survival and that of her offspring.

As we evolved and human development progressed, guaranteeing paternity or child survival was no longer required to the same degree. Relationships developed that were not only about children but also about emotional connection, support, and love. No longer did people need to be so fearful about the survival of their offspring or themselves, as many parts of the world had developed to a stage where danger, sickness, or starvation were not such regular problems. Reasons for jealousy evolved as well. The fear of lineage continuation, while still there, evolved into a fear of losing the relationship, or in emotional terms, the fear of being hurt, abandoned, losing power, or feeling sad about the loss of the relationship (whether it be a romantic relationship or even a friendship). Therefore, jealousy often arises at the idea of losing a relationship or the hurt that comes with betrayal by a partner. Jealousy is an attempt to prevent or block the emotional pain of hurt or grief. As most of us know, a jealous partner who becomes controlling to prevent their pain will likely push their partner away and thus add to the pain they are trying to avoid. Other people may use jealousy as an excuse to become violent. If such a person was able to be okay with the thought of being hurt or sad, they would be able to trust their partner and thus focus on building the fulfilling relationship they desire—one which was not about control but rather the meeting of mutual needs of both through compromise. If they happened to get hurt or lose the relationship in the process, it would reveal the quality of the relationship, or at least the emotional ability of one of the partners to maintain a loving, equal relationship for better or worse.

The second form of jealousy has less to do with relationships and more to do with one's own level of self-worth and self-acceptance. How often have you wished for something another person has? Perhaps it was money, a house, a relationship, a special ability, or perhaps it was something as small as a pair of shoes the person was wearing. When you saw they had something you desired, you might have felt the emotion of jealousy about it. A sense of unfairness that they had it and you did not. This type of jealousy can be helpful as it can highlight what it is you want and feel you are lacking. It can also be motivating to a person to chase what it is they think they lack and to persevere until they get it. Jealousy in this case can be beneficial as it will help a person recognize something they want and motivate them to do something to get it.

Problems with this type of jealousy occur for two reasons. The first is that the person feeling jealous continues to project jealousy toward whoever has what they want, when what they are really feeling is a sense of sadness, unworthiness, or dissatisfaction within themselves about not having something. Thus, jealousy masks their sadness about perceived or actual lack in their life. It has nothing to do with the other person and what they have.

The second reason is that to feel complete or happy we think we must always have more. The sense of only being happy when I get something is contrary to self-acceptance. When we can accept ourselves as we are, with or without whatever it is we desire, we will feel a sense of peace within despite our possessions both internal and external, and therefore be less inclined to feel jealous, sad, or less worthy about not having something.

While jealousy is a secondary emotion, it can be useful if it is used in a beneficial way to highlight what it is you want and improve your beliefs about your sense of lacking, especially in yourself. Much of the time, it is only trying to prevent us from feeling a primary emotion, and thus controlling another's behaviors in a way that can be detrimental to meaningful and healthy relationships. The ability to surrender to or accept the possibility of hurt or loss, to grieve the sadness or dissatisfaction about actual or perceived lack, or to accept yourself as you are, will minimize jealousy and assist you in making clearer decisions and dealing with the real issue.

Here are some other emotions which function similarly to jealousy:

- envious
- green-eyed
- possessive

Here are some other emotions with similar functions to compersion:

- calm
- at ease
- peaceful
- accepting

Creating an aligned pathway to deal with jealousy:

- Notice when you feel jealous. Look to see which type it is. Are you worried about being hurt or losing a relationship? Or is this more about you feeling sad about your sense of lack?
- Look out for feelings of sadness, hurt, rejection, fear, dissatisfaction, low self-worth, abandonment (or any other of the emotions we have discussed). These emotions are often underneath jealousy. Track the jealousy back to the primary emotion(s). Also be on the lookout for anger; it often comes after you feel jealous.
- Once you have understood the primary emotion(s) connected to jealousy, utilize the strategies taught in the book to help you cope with them.
- Connect to your true self using the techniques already discussed.
- Allow yourself to feel jealous; make peace with the sensations. It is normal to feel it. It is your mind's way of

trying to prevent sadness or to make you aware of your desires. Thank it for trying to help.

- Let go of any jealousy egoic thoughts such as: *I cannot trust them. They will leave me. I deserve to have that. It should be mine. Why do they have it and not me?* Thank your mind and recognize the thoughts as your mind's attempt to prevent or stop the painful emotions.
- Practice self-acceptance, self-appreciation, appreciation, self-compassion, self-respect, self-forgiveness, self-trust, and courage.
- Find or create some lighter thoughts.
- Ask yourself: Am I willing to trust this person? Am I willing to take the chance of being hurt to create the meaningful relationship I want? Is it okay to feel sad or not good enough because I do not yet have what I want? Am I still full and complete without it?
- Move on and live your life as fully and richly as possible. Yes, you feel jealous, sad, not good enough, and may feel hurt, but do you want to let this take over your whole life? Decide what feels true in the situation.

***

As a rule of thumb, the anger family is the family of emotions that we use to get rid of any unwanted emotions. If you feel the anger emotions, it will be useful to ask: *What emotion is the anger trying to protect me from feeling? What emotions are underneath this anger?*

***

If anger is related to the fight response, and anxiety to the flight response, the best way to describe the next set of resistance emotions designed to keep emotions to a level our ego can manage is to relate it to the freeze response.

Chapter Seventeen

The Freeze-Response Family of Emotions

Sensitive/Numb

When emotions become too strong for us, due to our sensitivity to them, many times our body goes into a state of shock, freezing, and disassociation as a coping strategy to avoid feeling the pain. This is what we call numbness. It is a state where things seem surreal and as if they are not happening and we feel disconnected from our emotional states. We may feel bland and neutral about the situation or ourselves. Numbness usually results in a lack of physical sensation and an absence of emotion. Perhaps we may feel the numbness as if we have been given anesthetic.

Numbness holds an important role in our functioning. It can help us to cope in an emotion-triggering situation when reacting emotionally would not serve us. It assists us in not falling apart and getting on with what needs to be done, even when things are emotionally difficult. From an evolutionary perspective, numbness would minimize our emotional pain in a traumatic life-threatening situation, thus allowing us to escape from it and deal with the pain at a time when we were safe. A most common time when we feel numb is when we are grieving. Stopping to grieve may not be practical, as there are many things that must be done, like planning a funeral or making decisions. Feeling numb as a coping mechanism dulls the emotions and makes functioning possible for us. On a smaller level, our boss may scream at us, but the numbness we feel may allow us to continue to do our work. Perhaps only later in the day does the real emotion of hurt arise, since we had felt numb initially as the coping strategy in the situation.

Numbness can also be a useful guide to assist us in determining what we are and what we are not sensitive to. We may feel numb to situations because they do not bother us, or we have experienced them so many times they do not create a reaction within us anymore. This type of numbness can also be of assistance, as always having to react to a situation emotionally may not serve us or change the situation, so we can move on more easily.

Numbness can be problematic for many reasons. Staying in a state of numbness disconnects us from our emotions, which can severely limit our motivation, inspiration, or impetus for action. It can also make it much harder to connect to our natural flow. We will find it difficult to make any decision about what is true to us when we do not have a connection to our emotions. Life can also seem bland with no emotion, like it has no flavor, thus resulting in an overall level of neutrality toward situations we may encounter, usually leading to a deep sense of dissatisfaction. Staying in numbness makes it extremely difficult to find what it is we do like and do not like and thus limits our overall life satisfaction.

Staying stuck in numbness is also a problem because underneath the numbness the emotions persist and thus become suppressed. Continually suppressing emotions will result in those emotions building up within us and then an eventual outpouring or becoming overly emotional. Staying in numbness also poses a problem for us because being disconnected from our emotions means we do not know when to act upon them. If, for example, a person feels numb to abuse they are facing, they are more inclined to stay and experience it, instead of acting in a self-protective way that the true self may be asking for. This type of numbness is often experienced by adults who were victims of emotional abuse as children. They are numb to the emotions of the abuse because it has served them to cope in the past, and thus they do not get triggered beyond their numbness and keep re-enacting the same relationships because they feel on familiar ground and are unable to feel the pain of the situation. Being numb to our emotions also disconnects us from our true self and therefore does not assist us in using our emotions to know when to change perceptions and help us make the best decisions aligned with our true self.

Numbness can sometimes be created by logical thinking. Being overly logical about everything, while creating a sense of expectedness and structure (which can create a sense of security for us), can also lead to feeling numb and lacking in emotion and any flare for creativity.

If numbness is serving you when it comes to getting through a difficult situation, then keep using it, but set aside some time to delve into your emotions to see what you are really feeling underneath it. If numbness is also helping you to live your truth, then continue to use it too. If it is suppressing your emotions or stopping you from living and connecting to yourself, it will be extremely useful for you to regularly check in with yourself to see how you feel underneath the numbness. Often, emotions in the anger and anxiety family are the first to appear when numbness starts to subside.

Numbness as an emotion also holds a special place for me. Being a habitually logical person, it is from the point of numbness that I was able to learn my emotions and allow myself to learn what it was like to feel and be free to live as my true self.

Other emotions with a similar function to numbness:

- detached
- shocked
- apathetic
- hollow
- indifferent

Other emotions with a similar function to sensitive:

- feeling any other emotion
- sensitive to feeling any other emotion
- empathic

Creating an aligned pathway to deal with numbness:

- Notice when you feel numbness. Look inside to see how you really feel. Start with little events that you think would normally trigger an emotion.
- Look out for feelings within the anger and anxiety family. Then look for sadness, hurt, rejection, embarrassment, guilt, disappointment, abandonment (or any other of the primary emotions we have discussed). These emotions are often underneath numbness. Track the numbness back to the primary emotion(s).
- Once you have understood the primary emotion(s), utilize the strategies taught in this book to help you cope with them.
- Connect to your true self using the techniques already discussed.
- Allow the numbness to exist; make peace with the sensations. It is normal to feel it. It is your mind's way of numbing the pain so you can cope. Thank it for trying to help.
- Let go of any numbness egoic thoughts such as: *It is what it is. There's nothing you can do about it. You can't change the past. I don't care.* Thank your mind and recognize the thoughts as your mind's attempt to prevent or stop the painful emotion.
- Practice self-love tools of self-appreciation, appreciation, self-trust, surrender, self-acceptance, and self-compassion.

- Find or create some lighter thoughts.
- Ask yourself: Is feeling numb helping me? If the answer is no, allow the feelings of pain to be, without trying to control them. If the answer is yes, allow the numbness to be there until you are ready to feel. The feelings may happen without you wanting them to, though.
- Move on and live your life as fully and richly as possible. Yes, you feel the emotions, but do you want to let them take over your whole life? Live your truth and start with something that brings about a little bit of pleasure.

Hopeful/Hopeless

Feeling hopeless is the internal sense of despair that nothing is going to change. We may physically feel drained or as if our vitality has been sucked out of us and feel we cannot go on another second, minute, hour, or day. Feeling hopeless is the opposite end of feeling hopeful. Hope keeps us moving forward no matter what obstacles may be in our way. Hope keeps us holding on to the chance that things will get better or improve to a level we are satisfied with. So, why do we have hopelessness?

Hopelessness as a tool or function is a useful emotion to assist us in facing certain realities—mainly the fact that some things may never change how we want them to. No matter how much we wish something or someone to be better, it may never happen. Thus, feeling hopeless can assist us in knowing when to give up trying or to make a decision to leave a current scenario as it will likely continue to stay the same.

Hope, on the other hand, is about holding on to the chance that things will improve, no matter how slight the chance may be. Maybe you will get the job, perhaps I will survive this cancer, maybe a miracle could occur, or my partner may still change. Hope will help us to continue trying or continue to move forward no matter what the trials, with the notion that the situation will get better eventually.

Therefore, hopelessness attempts to tell us when enough is enough, whereas hope tells us when to keep trying. The problem with both hope and hopelessness is that they both require our minds to predict the future. They require us to make an assumption of what will or will not happen and base our current decisions of action on that assumption. Unfortunately for us humans, we are not always good at making predictions. Few (if any) of us have a crystal ball at home that can tell us exactly what will happen. We will therefore often get it wrong in relation to things getting better or not.

Losing hope prematurely can result in calling it quits when it is still possible that things will improve. Life constantly changes, sometimes quickly, sometimes slowly. Many people who suffer through difficult times will make the prediction that things will not get better and thus feel hopeless. Many people with this belief can also often have suicidal ideation or make minimal efforts to improve the situation. Others may hold on to hope for too long. They will cling to the possibility that things will improve even when the evidence is pointing to the contrary, and thus suffer accordingly. Many people stay in marriages because they hope their partner will change. Or they remain in a job because they hope it will get better. They use hope as a form of denial of the current reality.

There is a fine balance which our true self sustains between holding out hope and feeling hopeless about a situation. Knowing when to use either emotion can assist in our daily life. In terms of hope, it can be useful to help us not to quit so easily. It can motivate us to explore the different options for improving our life or the situation at hand. It also leaves room for miracles or things to occur out of the scope of science or probability, thus helping us to forge ahead despite adversity. In terms of hopelessness, it can be a useful emotion to tell us when to quit or leave a situation after we have tried all possible options to fix or improve it but nothing has worked. In these scenarios, if a person holds on to hope for too long, they end up enduring much more suffering than if they had quit earlier.

The balancing point will be different for everyone. Before giving up hope and succumbing to hopelessness it is important to connect to our true self. If we feel our true self is motivating us to do something, it may want us to seek external help or information to gain knowledge we may need to make things better. If it still has not worked, maybe talking to a professional will help you to improve a situation. It is also important to give most things ample time to improve. Just because we want it to be better, it does not mean things will get better straight away.

Once you have tried everything you can over a period of time, then it may be time to contemplate the option of nothing changing and make your decision accordingly. Do I stay in the marriage? Can I continue to help my drug-addicted child? Taking away the hope does not mean things may not get better; it means things are unlikely to get better in my hands at this moment, and anything more I try to do or endure will likely result in my further suffering. So maybe you could accept the situation, then move in a clearer direction.

Hopelessness is a secondary emotion and will mostly come after long periods of feeling one of the other vulnerable emotions. It can also be useful to read about the emotion you are feeling underneath the hopelessness, as you learn to accept and allow that emotion and work with it.

Here are some other emotions with similar functions to hopelessness:

- despairing
- purposeless

- despondent
- resigned

Here are some other emotions with similar functions to hopeful:

- purposed
- encouraged
- excited

Creating an aligned pathway to deal with hopelessness:

- Notice when you feel hopeless.
- Check to see what emotions may be underneath hopelessness; some common ones are sad, hurt, dissatisfied, helpless. Learn how to deal with those specific emotions and use the steps for dealing with them.
- Connect to your true self using the techniques already discussed.
- Look out for suicidal ideation or any quitting/stopping thoughts. These are usual indicators of feeling hopeless.
- Allow yourself to feel the hopelessness; make peace with the sensations. It is normal for it to be there for you. It is your mind's way of trying to get you to either give up or change how you are doing something. Thank it for trying to help.
- Let go of any hopelessness found in egoic thoughts such as: *Things will never get better. Nothing will ever change. It will be like this forever. I'm better off dead.* Thank your mind and recognize the thoughts as your mind's attempt to get rid of your primary emotion, but acknowledge they are creating hopelessness.

- Practice self-love skills of compassion, self-appreciation, appreciation for life, and self-acceptance. Give self-encouragement, self-trust, and practice surrender.
- Find or create some lighter thoughts.
- Ask yourself: Does it feel true to me to give up in the situation, or continue to persevere and hope for more?
- Keep trying to live your life as fully and richly as possible each day. Yes, you feel hopeless, but do you want to let it take over your whole life? Focus on the here and now and do one thing per day that helps you to move forward a little or deal with the problem.

***

As you may realize by now, we have many emotions to help us live our lives from the truest possible place, and learning how to better relate to them in order to create more aligned action of the true self can minimize our time spent in the shadow emotions and enhance our ability to spend time in more of the light emotions. Knowing how to track our beliefs, emotions, and egoic behaviors can assist us in getting out of them more quickly.

Chapter Eighteen

Mindfully Tracking Emotional and Behavioral Pathways

To best live as our true self it is important to be aware of the current beliefs, emotions, and egoic behaviors with which we habitually engage. Being mindful of when and how they occur, as well as the order in which they arise, can give us greater insight into them. This enhances our ability to change them to align more closely with our true self using the skills you have learned in this book. Our most accessible entry into knowing if our beliefs are more or less aligned with our truth is our emotional states. Often, when we feel shadow emotions, particularly for long periods of time, it is an indication we are stuck in beliefs and egoic control patterns that do not reflect the true self. Our emotions and behaviors can be much easier to catch than our beliefs, so being aware of them is a great entry point into choosing to reconnect to our self.

Our emotions and reactions tend to be triggered in three different ways:

1. When we think about a situation from our past (an event that has occurred and is now over). For example, remembering being bullied in high school.
2. When a situation is occurring (a current event). For example, when your partner is not listening to you while you are speaking to them.
3. At the thought of a possible future situation (a situation that has not occurred). For example, worrying about losing your job.

Knowing which type of situation is triggering your emotions can make it easier to mindfully track your egoic patterns and then know what to do in that situation that aligns more with the calling of your true self.

For a past or current situation, the order generally works like this:

1. Core belief/perception about the situation...
2. Primary emotion(s)...
3. Conditioned egoic thoughts...
4. Secondary emotion(s)...
5. Conditioned egoic behaviors and more conditioned egoic thoughts...

Steps 3–5 can then continue to bounce off each other and create a spiral of suffering when they do not solve the primary emotions or if they do not align with our true selves.

While these combinations of emotions, thoughts, and behaviors change from person to person, an example of this type of pathway could look like the following.

Situation: Not being in a relationship

1. Core belief: *I'm not good enough unless I'm in a relationship.*
2. Primary emotions: sad, lonely and not good enough
3. Conditioned egoic thoughts: dwelling, questioning, if only/I wish, self-criticism
4. Secondary emotions: anger, jealousy, self-hate, hopelessness
5. Conditioned egoic behaviors: giving up, desperately searching for a partner, eating (trying to attain the light), avoidance of people in relationships

As you can see, the pathway started with the belief *I'm not good enough unless I'm in a relationship*. If the belief was in alignment with our true self, it would likely be *I am perfectly fine as I am, whether I have a relationship or not*. The pain of loneliness, feeling not good enough, and sadness shows that the belief is unaligned with our true self. If you are unable to notice the emotions you were feeling, you also have the ability to see your egoic behaviors (dwelling, questioning, giving up, overeating...) which would also point you back to that same belief.

When it comes to the prospect of a future situation it may look like this:

1. Mind views the situation as a possible threat that could trigger emotional or physical pain based on past experiences
2. Primary emotion (uncertainty, vulnerability, fear, or pressure)
3. Conditioned egoic thoughts (most likely worry, questioning or shoulds)
4. Resistance emotion(s)
5. Conditioned egoic behaviors (most likely avoidance, safety behaviors, or aggression) and more conditioned egoic thoughts

An example of this pathway could look like the following.

Situation: Meeting a new person

1. Beliefs: *The approval of others is necessary for me to approve of myself* or *People never like me when they meet me* or *I'm unlikeable.*
2. Emotion: uncertainty, fear, vulnerability, not good enough

3. Conditioned egoic thoughts (most likely worry or questioning): *What if I they don't like me? I could stuff up. I should choose my words carefully.*
4. Resistance emotion: anxiety
5. Conditioned egoic behaviors: avoid speaking, speak politely and avoid giving opinions, be agreeable, do not go to the meeting, leave early

Whenever we repeatedly engage in these future situations in this way, it will most often lead to us feeling dissatisfaction, regret, and/or disappointment.

Again, tracking our egoic behaviors, secondary emotions, or conditioned egoic thoughts along this pathway can lead us back to our belief patterns that do not necessarily align with those of our true self and lead us to more suffering, thus giving us the opportunity to change our beliefs and responses.

Aim to track your habitual pathways so you can respond from your inner truth and lighten your beliefs to be closer to that truer perception. Awareness of the pathway means that if we no longer need to use it, or use it flexibly, we can create new pathways that better align with our true self. Give yourself time to create these new pathways; they are not meant to create a new habitual, robotic response, but more as ways for you to discover how to connect to your true self, change your belief patterns, cope with emotions, and truly engage in aligned action at any given moment. Aligned action is dynamic and inspired and does not always seem logical, so it cannot be contained and bottled up into a one-size-fits-all model for all situations. The more you connect to your true self, the easier it will be to intuitively respond to situations and emotions in a more peaceful, healthy, and balanced way.

Chapter Nineteen

Your Way Forward

At this point you might expect yourself to have become a complete specialist in living your truth. You may have grown adept at recognizing and labeling emotions, you know how or when to use them, and you are skilled at recognizing and letting go of your conditioned egoic thoughts and behaviors. You may even be great at self-loving behaviors and creating lighter perceptions. You may also be great at tuning in to your inner being to listen to and act upon your truth. If this is the case, then great! My job is done, and I can give myself a big pat on the back.

Most likely, though, it is not the case, and that is fine too. I have still done my job and you are exactly where I am. That is, while I am able to put into practice everything I have written at times, I am still not perfect. I still fall out of the flow of the current of my river on occasion, but I use those times as opportunities to learn what swept me away and then realign to my truth. Getting to know our beliefs, emotions, behaviors, and our true self can take a whole lifetime, maybe even more! It is a journey of discovery, a journey of openness and honesty with ourselves. We are here living this thing we call life; none of us came here with a manual of how to live it. We did what we were taught, what we observed, and what we thought and felt was best. We stumbled and fell, and yet we still keep on moving. Sometimes we move at a faster place, other times at a slower pace; there is no right or wrong speed.

No matter how many times we have failed, no matter how much shadow we have experienced in our lifetime, we keep on moving; we keep on reconnecting to ourselves and chasing the light. While we may have doubts about the light at times, remember the shadow cannot exist without the light. Our shadow is always there attempting to push us forward, to help us to listen to deep within, to that inner part of us that is always whispering, to change our beliefs and move us toward our heart's truest desires. Always attempting to push us toward living the most peaceful, content, rich, and full life possible. A life of wellbeing that includes both shadow and light. A life of living your inner truth, moving with the flow of life.

It may help you to read this book several times. The information will sink into deeper and deeper levels of your consciousness. You will become more aware each time you read it, as the words become fully realized into your being. I personally still practice the strategies daily and come to greater insights all the time. Allow yourself to use it and come to deeper and deeper understandings of yourself in a kind and compassionate way.

No one can tell you what your truth is; it is your unique and individual flow. There is no one-size-fits-all way to live. Your job is to be *you*. It cannot be any other way. You are only able to live your life. There is no one else in the entire world who can live it for you, no one else who knows how to live your life, who knows how to be the spectacular individual you truly are. Connect to your inner being and be brave enough to be your true self and live your truth in a way no one else has the ability or knowledge to do. Your truth is yours to discover, it is yours to own, it is yours to enact, it is your gift to yourself and to the world.

Be the gift, accept your shadow, live in the light, and wake up to your self.

About Patrick Marando

Patrick Marando is a spiritual teacher and psychologist from Sydney, Australia with over 20 years of experience. His spiritual teachings revolve around bridging the gap between spirituality and psychology using his studies in Zen Buddhism, Taoism, Catholicism, New Age philosophies, and modern psychology, and focus on living from a state of truth. He had his first awakening experiences at the age of 28 and since that time his awakening has grown deeper and deeper. It is from his wealth of experience and knowledge that he continues to teach philosophies he himself discovered and outlined in this book.

A Message from Patrick Marando

Thank you for reading *Waking Up to Your Self*. My sincere hope is that you derived as much from reading this book as I did in creating it. If you have a few moments, please feel free to add a short review on your favorite online site for feedback. Reviews are very important for authors, and I truly appreciate each one. Also, if you would like to connect further with my teachings, please visit my website for news on upcoming works, events, recent blog posts, and to sign up for my newsletter: **www.patrickmarando.com**

Sincerely,
Patrick Marando

O-BOOKS

SPIRITUALITY

O is a symbol of the world, of oneness and unity; this eye represents knowledge and insight. We publish titles on general spirituality and living a spiritual life. We aim to inform and help you on your own journey in this life.
If you have enjoyed this book, why not tell other readers by posting a review on your preferred book site?

Recent bestsellers from O-Books are:

Heart of Tantric Sex
Diana Richardson
Revealing Eastern secrets of deep love and intimacy to Western couples.
Paperback: 978-1-90381-637-0 ebook: 978-1-84694-637-0

Crystal Prescriptions
The A-Z guide to over 1,200 symptoms and their healing crystals
Judy Hall
The first in the popular series of eight books, this handy little guide is packed as tight as a pill bottle with crystal remedies for ailments.
Paperback: 978-1-90504-740-6 ebook: 978-1-84694-629-5

Shine On

David Ditchfield and J S Jones

What if the aftereffects of a near-death experience were undeniable? What if a person could suddenly produce high-quality paintings of the afterlife, or if they acquired the ability to compose classical symphonies? Meet: David Ditchfield.

Paperback: 978-1-78904-365-5 ebook: 978-1-78904-366-2

The Way of Reiki

The Inner Teachings of Mikao Usui

Frans Stiene

The roadmap for deepening your understanding of the system of Reiki and rediscovering your True Self.

Paperback: 978-1-78535-665-0 ebook: 978-1-78535-744-2

You Are Not Your Thoughts

Frances Trussell

The journey to a mindful way of being, for those who want to truly know the power of mindfulness.

Paperback: 978-1-78535-816-6 ebook: 978-1-78535-817-3

The Mysteries of the Twelfth Astrological House

Fallen Angels

Carmen Turner-Schott, MSW, LISW

Everyone wants to know more about the most misunderstood house in astrology — the twelfth astrological house.

Paperback: 978-1-78099-343-0 ebook: 978-1-78099-344-7

WhatsApps from Heaven

Louise Hamlin

An account of a bereavement and the extraordinary signs — including WhatsApps — that a retired law lecturer received from her deceased husband.

Paperback: 978-1-78904-947-3 ebook: 978-1-78904-948-0

The Holistic Guide to Your Health & Well-being Today

Oliver Rolfe

A holistic guide to improving your complete health, both inside and out.

Paperback: 978-1-78535-392-5 ebook: 978-1-78535-393-2

Cool Sex

Diana Richardson and Wendy Doeleman

For deeply satisfying sex, the real secret is to reduce the heat, to cool down. Discover the empowerment and fulfilment of sex with loving mindfulness.

Paperback: 978-1-78904-351-8 ebook: 978-1-78904-352-5

Creating Real Happiness A to Z

Stephani Grace

Creating Real Happiness A to Z will help you understand the truth that you are not your ego (conditioned self).

Paperback: 978-1-78904-951-0 ebook: 978-1-78904-952-7

A Colourful Dose of Optimism
Jules Standish
It's time for us to look on the bright side, by boosting our mood and lifting our spirit, both in our interiors, as well as in our closet.
Paperback: 978-1-78904-927-5 ebook: 978-1-78904-928-2